BURNOUT
TO
BRILLIANCE

REDEFINING PEAK PERFORMANCE

JESS STUART

ISBN   978-0-9951425-2-7   (softcover)

ISBN   978-0-9951425-3-4   (kindle)

ISBN   978-0-9951425-4-1   (print on demand)

Other books by Jess Stuart:

A Rough Guide to a Smooth Life (2015)   9781504343817

Like a Girl (2018   9781973983460

The Superwoman Survival Guide (2020)   9780473517908

I Love Mondays (2021)   9780995142503

For Mum & Dad
who've always believed in my brilliance

CONTENTS

Our deepest fear is not that we are inadequate.
Our deepest fear is that we are powerful beyond measure. It is
our light, not our darkness, that most frightens us.

We ask ourselves, 'Who am I to be brilliant, gorgeous, talented,
fabulous?' Actually, who are you *not* to be?

Marianne Williamson

INTRODUCTION

When I first sat and thought about being our best and achieving the unique potential that's within us all 'brilliance' is the word that came to mind. It's the feeling we get when the sun lights up a room we're in, or the first glimpse of the sun over the horizon at sunrise. It's that light-bulb moment when we have an amazing idea and it's the lighting up of our life when we're living brilliantly. It's the five-star ratings on our performance when we're at our best, and it's the light that shines on others when we move through work and life being our brilliant self.

The words we use to describe brilliance are wide ranging. Here are a few of my favourites that highlight what I mean: cheerful, happy, lively, optimistic, bright, clear, dazzling, light, positive, smart, intelligent, sharp, quick, talented, inspired, skilful, excellent. These are the attributes we aim for when we aim for peak performance and the things we experience when we're at our best.

When we're brilliant, we shine. Light is an intrinsic part of the concept of being brilliant. In fact, it feels light to live this way, and when we're closer to burnout it feels like a darker place to be.

I love the light bulb metaphor for brilliance, and for me brilliance also represents energy, which is key to sustaining our brilliance. When we're at our best we have more energy, and like a light bulb we always shine brighter when we have more energy. Brightness is also synonymous with intelligence, and of course, when we're being brilliant our intellect is at its sharpest and our brains are functioning at their full capability.

When I was in Bhutan, the kingdom famous for measuring Gross National Happiness in place of Gross Domestic Product (GDP), I was surrounded by brilliance, in terms of the light emanating from the people and the priorities their government had around environment, culture and sustainability. Many of the temples I visited had rooms full of butter lamps; there always seemed to be lights burning bright. It is said in Buddhism that light is the knowledge that dispels the darkness of ignorance. This, for me, perfectly sums up this book.

How do we move from the ignorance of busyness and burnout to tap into our true potential and be brilliant?

I'm here to provide you with a roadmap for burning bright rather than burning out.

Allow me to take you on that journey. We'll start by looking at what got us here in the first place: why burnout is so prevalent and what we can do about it. I'll show you how to spot it, how to deal with it and how to continue to avoid it in the future.

This book isn't really a book about burnout, though: it's more about redefining peak performance and developing a roadmap for getting there.

We don't become brilliant just by avoiding burnout, yet burnout is one of the major barriers to peak performance, and something many of us struggle with.

Beyond surviving burnout, what can we do to achieve our potential? And does it have to come with exhaustion, stress and anxiety?

I believe not. This book is designed to take you on a journey from burnout to brilliance. To uncover you at your peak and create ways you can be your best without burning out in the process.

We'll not necessarily be talking about new concepts here; we'll be exploring new ways of looking at them. This book contains very practical strategies to apply what you learn alongside my own personal anecdotes and experiences from a decade spent coaching others. It will enable you to make change and to gain control, in a way that feels achievable and manageable. Let's face it: none of us have the capacity to be adding anything else to the to-do list, or making a long list of new things we need to feel guilty about not doing. This book is about working with what you have and working out a plan that suits you, because after all we're all different, and we're all capable of shining in our own unique way.

One of my extrovert friends prefers to shine in a room full of at least 100 people. I felt my light dim just hearing her talk about it! For me, my light is brightest when it's in a room alone. We're all different. Take what works for you from these pages: pick the things that resonate and are easy for you to achieve.

In this book, we'll explore some of our long-held beliefs about what makes us brilliant. We'll look at the concept that more is not always better – in fact, constantly striving for more may be the very thing contributing to our undoing. In fact, the visions we're sold on Instagram are not achievable or real, and our organisational ways of working are built on an outdated model intended for the industrial age.

The 'more is better' attitude has pervaded our society, and resulted in marketing messages that only get us into debt, a mania for comparison with others (keeping up with the Joneses) and even hangovers and obesity! It's an easy trap to fall into, and one I sometimes find myself in. A couple of wines on a Friday after work is great, but the whole bottle feels less great the next morning, when you wake up with a headache and a mouth like the bottom of a birdcage. We all love a slice of cake, but the 'more is better' mantra can lead to us eating the whole thing and feeling sick. More is not necessarily better, even for the things we enjoy.

This is why brilliance has become harder to attain. Towards the end of the book we'll explore some of the barriers that get in the way of us achieving brilliance.

But first, we'll start by exploring what got us here in the first place. Why are we so attached to busy? Why has it been sold to us as the pathway to success? We'll look at the different types of busy and learn the difference between busy and effective.

Given busyness can lead to burnout, we will visit this term and come to understand what it means. Most importantly, we'll learn how to spot it, how to deal with it and hopefully how to avoid it in future. This leads us nicely to the part of the book where we'll start building a plan for you: your roadmap towards brilliance.

I'll help you understand what makes you a sustainable resource, where your energy comes from and how to sustain it to keep your light shining. This includes resilience-building strategies and the role of self-care. It's important that we pause to consider the negative impacts the pressures around self-care have led to. It's almost become a badge of honour – every Instagram wellness warrior has us convinced we're falling short in this area! How has this changed as a result of the pandemic? Why has it become more of a challenge than it used to be? We'll uncover how we can make self-care achievable in way that works for us.

In the second half of the book, we'll take a closer look at the mindset required for brilliance, how to increase effectiveness and the habits that will help us achieve peak performance.

We'll learn how to deal with a busy brain and cultivate new thinking patterns that help us nurture our brilliance and recognise our potential.

I'll tell you about the concept of 'flow': what it looks and feels like, how we can get there more often and how it can help us do more of our best work. I'll teach you some strategies for when times get tough; about how to continue to shine in the darkest of times, manage change and weather the storms.

The concept of brilliance includes performing at our peak, but not in the way we often think. It's not about climbing a mountain and ending up at the top (the peak); it's more about riding the waves: peaking at regular intervals when it's required and resting in between.

When we are brilliant, we are performing at our peak, and tapping into our unique potential. I'll talk about how to understand what that potential is and how to access it.

When we're performing at our peak, we are resilient and we have the energy reserves we need. We are more effective so, the quality of what we're producing improves too.

To understand the relationship between potential, performance, resilience and brilliance, I'm going to use a light-bulb metaphor. Potential is the type of light bulb we are: our brand, our size, our shape and the purpose we connect to on our journey to becoming the best light bulb we can be. Performance is the action of that happening: switching on the light and doing the job – providing light in the darkness. Resilience is the energy that fuels that light to continue to shine (keep performing); it involves ensuring we don't leave it on too long or 'over-perform'. Brilliance is the brightness of the light: how well it shines. We know that a high-performing light bulb outshines others. We also know that if we leave it on too long, no matter how bright it is, it will eventually burn out.

This book is designed to be a compendium of current wisdom, with a fresh approach to long-held beliefs about busyness and performance, backed by my own personal story and presented alongside practical strategies and exercises designed to help you apply what you're learning as you go.

By the end of this book, you'll have a fresh approach to ensuring you are a sustainable resource, equipped with knowledge on how you can reenergise and go from burnout to brilliance. I aim to take away those sticks you so often use to beat yourself up with, and help you see there is a way of doing less to achieve more. That brilliance is about quality, not quantity. I'm going to tell you why we've been getting busyness all wrong, and how to fix that.

My wish for you, reading this book is for you to shine bright, to shine your light on others and to ensure that light never goes out.

MY OWN BURNOUT

I was born in rural England to a loving family. We were not well off, but my life was generally one of privilege. I was sold on the cultural norms of being a high-achieving woman. I climbed the career ladder, and chased the promotions, the company car and the salary package. I got the top job and the beach house. I settled down and had it all figured out by the age of 30 – or so I thought. I was working hard and yet there was always more to do, more to prove. It was never enough.

The result was that I became stuck on the treadmill of 'doing' life without really finding any joy in it. I wasn't living my life, and as a result I was deeply unfulfilled. I'd lost touch with what was important, who I was and what I wanted. My health began to suffer, and I was unhappy – it was at that point I experienced burnout.

It was shortly after I'd taken over covering the role of a colleague in addition to my own. Now heading up two teams and looking after 10 sites instead of five, I was stretched further across the country, sitting in more leadership meetings and involved in more projects than I could keep up with.

I spent most days in the car or back-to-back meetings. I had little time to enjoy the beach house I had settled in, as I was always in hotels working away. When I was at home, I had little time or energy to indulge in any hobbies or exercise, or even function in my relationship. But the high achiever in me kept pushing. More was better: I had to prove myself, and failure was not an option. Besides, I didn't want to let people down.

My boss at the time called me to ask if I'd manage a big change project about to hit the manufacturing part of the business. I was going through a breakup with my partner of seven years, and she thought it might 'help take my mind off it'. It was the straw that broke the camel's back. As my life unravelled, so did my health.

Physically, the defining moment came at a gym class on my 31st birthday. I was exhausted as usual and a little out of shape, but also looking for excuses not to go home and face the music. Midway through a step class, I felt a pop in my knee and collapsed to the floor. Amid the thumping music and frowns of onlookers, I broke down and cried, heaving sobs. I couldn't even feel my knee, so it wasn't pain-related; it was the fact that a lid of emotions seemed to have had lifted, and it hit me like a truck. I started to cry that night, and didn't stop for about a month. I couldn't get out of bed, and conveniently for my work I was bedridden for recovery of my ruptured cruciate, which might need surgery. For work purposes I could hide behind this sports injury rather than my breakdown. I didn't want anyone to know I'd failed; that I couldn't cope, couldn't keep up.

Those long days in bed gave me a lot of time to think, and forced me to spend time recovering because there wasn't much else I could do. I also started to talk to a professional about what was really going on for me, in a bid to figure out what I should do next.

That turned out to be to wipe the slate clean and start again. To throw out everything that wasn't working and figure out what would. My relationship, my job – even the beach house – all ended so I could begin the rebuild and finally devote time to who I was and what I wanted.

I knew something had to change, and decided that that 'something' was everything.

My reinvention wasn't a revelation that came to me in the middle of the night during a 'seeing the light' moment. It was more of a 'hitting a brick wall' kind of moment: I hit the wall, and then the wall came crashing down on top of me. It was a choice my body helped me make, because it realised after a year of hints that I wasn't getting the message.

When I think back, the signs were there. It was a slow burn; it was just always more convenient for me not to notice. I was always on the verge of getting sick, battling a tiredness no amount of sleep or long weekends could cure. My batteries always seemed to be running on empty, and I'd lost my motivation for practically everything. I didn't have any joy in my work, or in the things I used to enjoy in life. I'd excuse this malaise at the weekend, telling myself I was tired and rest was the right thing to do to offset the busyness, and then I'd throw myself into my work to keep my mind off these gnawing doubts and problems.

I withdrew from friends, as I hadn't the energy to socialise. I justified it by telling them how big and important my job was, and in my own head told myself I needed the rest and that those with 'my sort of job' couldn't be expected to socialise in the week; it wasn't part of the deal. The truth was I'd lost interest in being around others or having fun or making an effort to do anything really. The irony was that this big job that took up so much of my life and was the Holy Grail of career success actually no longer interested me either. I'd lost my passion for the very thing I was making all these sacrifices for. I didn't want to be at work; I couldn't really care less about the work I was doing, such was my burnout. In hindsight I can see that I was checking out, losing motivation and ultimately disengaging from work and life because of my burnout.

I'd got into the habit of drinking a bottle of wine every Friday to unwind, and got out of the habit of exercise. Before my burnout that would be another thing I'd cram in so my life had all the hallmarks of success. I'd go to 6 am yoga or head to the gym after work but just prior to my burnout even that had slipped: I'd treat myself to takeaways because I had no energy to cook and, well, I needed a treat. Life was hard – this was self-care, wasn't it?

I'd tell myself I could do more self-care when my holidays rolled around, but of course it was never the right time to take leave, so they never did come around.

So, at 31, I gave it all up and started again, in a bid to recover from my burnout and to ensure that I never got this low again. I wanted to rebuild my life around my passions. If plan A wasn't the answer, as everyone had led me to believe, what was?

I walked away from my long-term relationship, gave up my career in the corporate world and decided on a complete change of direction: I would follow my passion for writing books.

Part of my recovery included a trip to Bali (isn't that where everyone goes when they burn out?) and another part involved spending time back in the UK with those who I loved and needed around. I interspersed these with many retreats and ashram stays, at which I could devote time to yoga, mindfulness, silence, meditation and reconnecting with myself.

This turned out to be the turning point.

I spent a year writing my first book and doing other things that made my heart sing, including travelling the circumference of Australia in a camper van and visiting Bhutan. I taught English to Buddhist monks in Thailand, and lived in ashrams and mindfulness centres.

I had always been sold on the concept that a good job and a regular income provides you with reliability. It's scary not to have a pay cheque coming into your account every month, and for me it was the first time I wasn't earning since I had been old enough to work.

I returned to New Zealand as a qualified coach, yoga teacher and mindfulness practitioner, with no money in my bank account. This is how I began the next chapter of my life. Based in Wellington, where I didn't know anyone, I began putting on events, coaching and writing my second book, sharing what I'd learned and my passion with others. Within six weeks, I met the woman who is now my wife, and by the end of the year, I had a second book, a business, a new home and a dog!

In hindsight, I realise that, during my time in the corporate world, I burnt out because I was too busy trying to prove myself and looking after everyone else around me. I was juggling too many things and trying to make them all perfect, yet barely keeping up. I'd beat myself up for not having the energy to go to the gym or get up early for yoga before work. I spent a lot of hours travelling and in meetings – earning a living but not making a life.

However, my time in the corporate world provided me with some valuable research for the work I do now. I noticed some recurring themes as I worked in human resources (HR) with leadership teams across multiple countries and industries. Being in HR, you have a unique position, in that you're often the coach and confidante of senior leaders. Not only do you get to sit on the leadership team; you also get to be privy to the recruitment to the team, and to talent and performance conversations.

This, combined with my own involvement in sport as a captain and player across Rugby, Football and Netball teams, led me to a fascination with peak performance. How do we sustain it? What is the difference between those who can and those who don't? I saw that it wasn't about capability, as we often think. It was much more about our mindset, our habits and the *way* we did what we did.

My journey has come full circle. I find myself drawing on skills from my corporate HR days of coaching, personal development, leadership development and training, now with the added benefit of my years in studying mindfulness and understanding balance, authenticity and the recipe for fulfilment.

MIND YOUR BUSYNESS

Let's explore what got us here in the first place.

I want to begin by articulating a case for change and discussing how our current ways of working have failed us. Why do so many of us feel closer to burnout than brilliance? Once we understand this, we'll be able to learn how to navigate the problem and create change.

Let's discover why we're so attached to busy. I'll take you through the impacts and costs of this attachment, as well as what we can do about it. In this chapter we'll look at the different types of busy, the difference between busy and effective and the power of language. We'll be discussing our perception of time, and the things we can tell ourselves to allow us to be productive and effective and work in a way that gives us control and helps us produce our best.

We know all about the concept of a pandemic these days. We're living in the context of a pandemic that is widely covered by the media, and disliked and feared by most. However, we're also living in the context of *another* pandemic that has secretly been waging a war on our modern society. The problem with this one is that there's no test or vaccine. It flies under the radar. Everyone seems to be infected, and it has been actively encouraged as a positive across our organisations.

I am talking about busyness: our need to be busy to feel productive; our fear that if we're not busy we're not doing enough; and our belief that the busier we are the more we must be contributing, therefore the closer we are to success.

The busyness pandemic has led to the prevalence of burnout in our society – and the irony is it takes us further away from the success we've been led to believe it brings.

When researching my last book, I asked my followers to describe their life in one word. Over 50 per cent said 'busy' or some close descriptor ('crazy', 'full', 'chaotic'). It's no wonder burnout and mental health issues are on the rise when so many of us live such busy lives with crazy schedules. It leads to a feeling of chaos and overwhelm that affects our ability to perform – and, ultimately, our health.

We live in a world where busyness is worn like a badge of honour, and the busier we are the more successful we must be – at least that's what we tell ourselves.

Yet we're all rushing through life with anxiety and stress trailing behind us, lacking sleep and in a state of constant worry. We have no time to rest, to breathe or to do the things we love with the ones we love.

We attach our sense of self-worth to being busy. Being busy means we're valued, needed and successful. As a result, we've deprioritised balance, rest and downtime. We've been taught not to see these things as effective, when really they should be our foundation. Balance, rest and downtime are where it all starts. Without them, we end up burning out.

A few years ago a friend of mine received a cancer diagnosis out of the blue. When the doctor asked her if she'd had any symptoms or felt tired, she said, 'Yeah, I'm tired, but I've got three kids and I run my own business.' It's almost like we feel this kind of fatigue is normal, rather than a sign from our body that something is wrong.

We live like our purpose is to get everything done: the to-do list wiped clean and the inbox empty. But even when we die, there will still be things on our to-do lists, and the world won't end – someone else will do them.

We live like life is one big emergency, and we tell ourselves we'll relax and take a break 'when it's done' – but it never is. As fast as we tick off things we've done, more things we need to do emerge.

So much of what we put on our to-do list, both at home and at work, we treat like an emergency: it must get done; it's critical that the report gets finished or I make that meeting or deliver this presentation. I must get to the gym tonight and do my class; it's imperative the cakes for the school morning tea are baked tonight, and I need to pick up ingredients on the way home.

If some of this doesn't get done, would it be the end of the world? How much of our to-do list will matter five years from now? Unless we're a doctor, a nurse or fighting to free a hostage, much of what we do at work is not life or death, so why do we behave like it is?

How much of our to-do list really needs our immediate attention, or is so important we must put it before our children, our partner and our health?

Our busyness is one of the reasons so many of us feel overwhelmed. The feeling that we need to be busy to be of value, worthy and successful keeps us on this treadmill, even when it's impacting our health.

THE POWER OF LANGUAGE AND PERCEPTION

The language we use and the way we respond to others or talk to ourselves will determine how we feel. People are constantly telling me how busy they are, even if they're not! When we are constantly saying 'I'm so busy', our brain looks for evidence to make it true, then we begin to feel overwhelmed. What you say is what you get.

When you ask someone how their day has been, you often get the response 'busy' – even if they've not been busy. It's a term we've come to associate with success and productivity. We also believe the opposite of busy is not a good thing to confess to, particularly at work. Of course, we all have different set points where busy is concerned and for some this means a bigger quantity than others. It is true for us all, though, that if we continually say we're busy we're telling our overwhelmed, stressed minds there's too much going on. We're buying into the very thought patterns that are making us feel overwhelmed in the first place and evidencing that stress in the brain. This mental stress can then go on to affect us physically.

Whilst we're on the subject of language, let's talk about another dangerous word that makes us busy: 'should'. This one plays into our busyness by placing a whole lot of things on our to-do list we feel obliged to do for others or because of how we'll be perceived if we don't. I *should* do this for a colleague, or for my kids, or because it's expected of me. I *should* work late because my boss is working late. I *shouldn't* leave at 3 pm because no one else does and they'll think I'm lazy, even though I started at 7 am.

Our need to be busy or controlled by the *shoulds* often comes from a place of scarcity. There's never enough time in the day, so we get busy to try and achieve more.

It's frequently our perspective of time driving the busyness: we have a constant feeling we're running out of time, so we need to be busy to fit everything in. There never seems to be enough time in our schedules.

Aside from the rhythms of nature (sunrise and sunset and the turning of the seasons), we have created the calendar, the 24-hour day, the clock and the nine-to-five. These human-defined concepts change depending on which country you're in and what traditions you follow. It's why the first of January is not the New Year for everyone.

To this extent, time is a made-up concept.

If that is the case, it means we get to define what time means to us. (Within reason, of course. I get that this is easier to get to grips with if we work for ourselves and we're not restricted to someone else's schedule; for example, a series of company meetings.)

The way we view time is in our control, and the quantity of time we're viewing is the same amount, whether we're looking at hours in the day or hours in our lifetime (regardless of how long that is). We either look at each hour or day as one less, or one more.

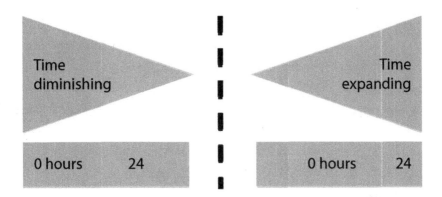

Our view of time can be of time opening up or time decreasing, from the starting point to the end: an 80-year lifespan, a 365-day year or the 24 hours we all have in a day. It's the same block of time we're taking about: we can choose the lens through which we view it.

If I'm constantly telling myself there are not enough hours in the day, that's how I'll feel. Yet we all have the same 24-hour block every day. Every day after we wake up, we can see each hour as either an hour less we have in the day or an hour more.

We get to choose how we relate to time and whether we feel we've got enough of it or not. I believe our problem with time is not that we have so little of it, but rather that we waste too much of it.

We can't find 10 minutes a day to meditate, but we frequently spend 10 minutes scrolling on Facebook, and when we're done we can't even remember what we looked at. I can't find a couple of hours in the evening to do that online course, but I can often find the time to binge-watch a Netflix series I don't even like that much.

Does your schedule align to your priorities? There's a school of thought that we always have time for something if it's important:

we make the time. So our schedule is less about time and more about priorities.

I might not have time to play ball with the dog when I'm responding to emails, but if she trod on a nail and came limping into the office, you bet I'd find the time to remove the nail – same time, different priorities.

Another helpful way of looking at time is to break it down into blocks. Often, there are small blocks of time between activities that we can use. We're not usually intentional about those small blocks: we use them to scroll on our phones, rechecking our emails or gossip by the water cooler. If we're not intentional about how we use our time, it's much easier to waste precious moments of it.

If we divide our 24-hour day into 20-minute blocks, we'll find we've got 72 of them. That sounds like a lot. Granted, three of those blocks will be taken up with a meeting. Many more make up our hours of sleep. But some of them will be blocks of 20 minutes between activities that we could sensibly use. What do we choose to do with those blocks? When we say we haven't had time for exercise, to get outside or to put our meditation app on today, here's the solution. Carve out those 20-minute blocks of time, and consciously choose what to do with them.

Changing how we think of time and how we glorify 'busy' is fundamental, because our beliefs determine our experience.

On the subject of our language and our perception of time, I love Dr Libby Weaver's suggestion. When we find ourselves saying, 'I have to do this,' we put a negative slant on the task, because we're busy and overwhelmed. Yet a lot of what we 'have' to do, we choose to do, and we'd be disappointed if we couldn't do it. This represents an opportunity to reframe our language.

I complain about having to go to the gym, but when I think about times when I've been injured and unable to get off the sofa, I realise I'd have given anything then to have been able to move freely without pain and be fit again.

Whether it's going to the gym, studying for exams or picking the kids up from school, Dr Libby advises we switch our language from 'I have to' to 'I get to'. I've tried it, and it works.

I get to go to the gym, because I'm fit and healthy and I can walk. I get to pick the kids up from school, because I'm lucky enough to have been able to have kids. I live in a country where they get an education, and I can afford to send them to school.

Can you see how this shifts our feelings about these things we choose to do? Each activity is not another chore on our list but something we're lucky to get to choose.

So next time you're feeling like you have to do something, flip the narrative – 'I get to'.

Language is so important, because if we tell ourselves something often enough, our mind will believe it's true. That's why if we tell ourselves and everyone around us we're stressed and busy all the time, our minds will become overwhelmed.

Now we've established our control over time and our ability to create a new perspective, let's look at other reasons for busyness.

TYPES OF BUSY

Let's explore the different types of busy and the impacts they can have. Whilst busyness has been made fashionable, it presents in different ways and therefore has varying effects.

When we've got 'busy' right, it's achievable, it's aligned to our skill set and it gives us a sense of purpose. It presents us with just enough of a challenge, whilst still delivering a sense of accomplishment (i.e., not so much of a challenge that we have to work 80-hour weeks to meet it).

At its best, good 'busy' is a healthy rhythm that equates to performance. Unfortunately, most often this is not the case.

Sometimes we're busy over-delivering, trying to prove ourselves because we lack confidence and fear we're going to get found out – this is the insecure type of busy often associated with feeling like an imposter. We experience a pressure to know all the answers which keeps us busy chasing after perfect outcomes. This is common in high achievers and perfectionists.

Or we're just the kind of busy that thrives on chaos, being needed and wanting to do it all so we can complain about the stress we're under, a martyr of busy. The result is often under-performance but at its worst becomes overwhelm, avoidance and procrastination.

We can be so worried we'll fail that we don't even try, or the pressure to know more stops us from making the smallest progress or making a start. Or we've got problems we'd rather avoid, so busyness becomes a great distraction. I can safely say that, during my career, I've been all of these types of busy at one time or another.

BUSY TYPE	RESULT	BEHAVIOUR	
PERFORMER	PRODUCTIVE	CONFIDENCE	I'm effective
HIGH ACHIEVER	OVER DELIVERS	PERFECTIONIST	I need to do more No-one will do it like I can
IMPOSTER	NOT ENOUGH	SELF-DOUBT	I need to prove myself I'm going to get found out
MARTYR	STRESS/CHAOS	BUSY BADGE OF HONOUR	Needs to be needed Who'll do it if I don't?
AVOIDER	PROCRASTINATE	DISTRACTED	Worried I might fail so don't try Need to know more before I begin Don't want to face my problem

What type of busy are you?

Understanding why we behave the way we do and the resulting impact is the first step to doing something about it.

For many of us, the reason we're so busy comes from expectations our society has created, our attachment to busy as a marker of self-worth and our belief the busier we are the more we'll achieve and the closer to success we'll get.

ARE YOU BUSY OR EFFECTIVE?

Once we know what drives our busyness, the next question to ask is whether you are busy or effective. The two are very different. We can understand this more fully by further exploring the difference between quantity and quality.

This is an interesting question, because most of us have been conditioned to believe that the busier we are the more productive we'll be.

Being productive is often about the amount we produce, but being effective is the critical element here. We all want to be productive at work. For many organisations, productivity programmes have been all the rage over the last couple of decades. Effectiveness is not just about increasing what we produce, though; the *output*, as the term 'productivity' suggests. It's also about the quality of the output.

The term 'productivity' reminds me of my days in manufacturing, when we'd refer to the amount of product that had come off the line. If you're making buckets, the more that come off the line, the better, right? The more orders you fill and the more money you make. Unless those buckets have holes in them, or other manufacturing defects. The amount is not always the point: that's why I prefer to use 'effectiveness' in place of 'productivity'. I know that we're humans, not buckets, so we work a bit differently. The point is that effectiveness is all about the quality of what we're producing.

We live in a world that prioritises quantity over quality – we think that more is always better. The more hours we work, the more valued we will be as an employee, the more successful we'll be and the more we'll earn – it's where the concept of the hourly rate came from.

Since the industrial revolution, we've measured performance in a way that suggests more is better. We are paid for every hour we work and not a penny more or less, regardless of the quality of what we produce during those hours.

This theory works up to a point – until we burn out. Then, we're not effective or valuable to anyone.

The focus in our world is on quantity, multitasking and doing more things in less time. At the same time, we've been conditioned to believe that 'pushing through' is a sign of strength and a prerequisite for success It's not a coincidence burnout has become so prevalent.

The current system is an outdated model we used to run our factories during the industrial age. It's a model that rewards time spent, not quality achieved.

I'd like us to flip the narrative on this, and understand more is not necessarily better, especially where performance is concerned. We can work hard, but only to a point. Without the necessary balance, including downtime, the hard work starts to become ineffective.

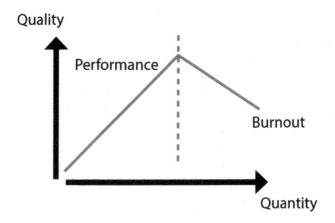

We hit a point at peak performance where further quantity starts to affect the quality of what we produce. This is the point at which we're more likely to make mistakes, less likely to innovate and less tolerant with those we're working with. At this point the pursuit of quantity starts to decrease our effectiveness, until we eventually hit burnout.

If we can do enough to hit peak performance without doing so much that we lose our effectiveness, we've hit the sweet spot. This leads to less overwhelm and burnout, and ensures we are a sustainable resource.

So how do we strike the balance and ensure we don't hit that tipping point? How do we become effective, and battle the busyness in a way that ensures we remain so?

Again, it comes back to this concept of more is not always better, quality brings about better results than quantity.

In his book, *Essentialism*, Greg Mckeown talks about this concept of less but better. He tells us the word priority is a singular and always was in our language, dating back to the 1400s, it's only since the 1900s we see it used as a plural; priorities. Our struggle today is that we often have too many priorities when there should just be one. By nature of its definition there should only be one priority. Mckeown is an advocate for focusing on one thing to enable to give that the best of our attention.

It's how we spread our energy across our tasks and this diagram shows how we can dilute our progress if we have too many priorities. Using the same reserve of energy across multiple tasks reduces the progress of each rather than putting all our energy on one thing.

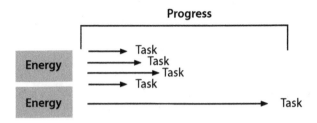

Going from being spread too thin trying to do it all but achieving nothing to doing what matters and nailing it. It's less about doing more things and more about doing the *right* things.

So what's your one thing? What's the right thing to make your priority?

I find it helpful when faced with a busy to do list or an ambitious set of goals to ask myself "what if I could only do one, which would it be?"

The majority of people I speak to about this say they don't have time, and that's the whole problem. But the fact we are too busy to take time out to relax is the precise reason it's so important we do. In a world that encourages noise and busyness, we find it so hard to be quiet and still, yet quiet and stillness are a necessary part of good health and building resilience.

Our attachment to busy has meant we've deprioritised downtime and pauses and endeavoured to remove them from our lives, because we see them as a waste of time when we could be doing something 'productive'. By trying to maximise every second of every day, we've removed all opportunities to rest and recharge, and have no space left in our lives.

Self-care is often viewed as a nice-to-have: something to do when we get a spare few minutes or when the to-do list is done. It's something we leave until we've got time and don't prioritise when we're busy. The irony is this is the time we probably need it most.

We worry that taking some downtime might be seen as selfish, lazy or unproductive. Yet it's critical in helping us build resilience and perform at our peak.

If you take time out for yourself, it won't only be you who benefits. Imagine what a better partner, parent and worker you'd be if you weren't stressed and tired – how much more you could give others and how much better your relationships would be. Taking time out for yourself is anything but selfish; everyone will benefit from a better, more refreshed you.

This is a concept I refer to as slowing down to speed up. I know it sounds counterintuitive, but bear with me.

If we slow down by taking small pauses in our day to recharge and press reset, we'll be more effective when we return to our day. If we are clear-headed and well-rested, we function better. We get things done more quickly, navigate setbacks with ease and have more space to innovate. All of this together means that, by slowing down, we are in fact speeding up, by becoming more effective and sharper and performing at our peak.

It sounds like it'll take longer, but this process is like stopping to put petrol in the car on a long journey. It takes a few minutes to pull over and stop, but doing so means we can go further. If we didn't take those few minutes to fill up, we'd break down on the way and not arrive at our destination.

We need to start seeing self-care and time out as a must-have – a priority. Not a nice-to-have, luxury item reserved for when we've got time, when the to-do list is complete – because it never is. If we take time out, make sure we feel rested and refreshed, get a good night's sleep, take the time to exercise and eat right, we can perform better. This means things don't take as long: we've got more energy, we can make decisions and solve problems quicker, we make fewer mistakes and we get it done right the first time.

Self-care is something I talk about a lot, and something we'll expand on in coming chapters. It's become one of my non-negotiables. I learned this lesson the hard way, back in the corporate world, when the busier I thought I was, the more valued I felt.

The more hours I worked, the more status I achieved and the more money I earned, the happier I thought I'd be. It turns out this isn't the formula. Whilst I'm still busy these days, I've mastered the art of balance and flow.

All Blacks skills coach Gilbert Enoka talks about performance waves. Waves come in sets. For the All Blacks, the peak of the wave should be game day, when they push hard, compete and perform. But, Enoka says, this always needs to be followed by recovery time, a rest day: the calm water or trough before the next wave. Trying to perform at the peak of the wave all the time simply isn't sustainable. To get to the peak, we must also experience the trough: in fact, it's the troughs that prepare us for the peaks. As a surfer, I know how much energy it takes to paddle out, catch a wave and surf it in. We can't spend the whole session doing this. We need the troughs in between waves to recover.

The bottom line is that the more we do in a day, the less we'll do well, because this activity is coupled with a sense of overwhelm and exhaustion and, as a result, we can't be at our best. We perform best when we're rested, refreshed and not stressed.

I've learned that this is fundamental to my success. This is why I prioritise self-care. It makes me more effective, and it means I can get more done. If we don't make time for self-care, we will need to make time for illness.

In a world where burnout and overwhelm are so common, being busy may not be the gold star we've been led to believe. Being busy does not mean we're effective; in fact, it could mean the opposite.

It's this difference between quantity and quality which is also the difference between being busy or effective. In fact, the busier we are the less effective we're likely to be.

BURNOUT BASICS

Now we've set the scene on busyness, let's look a little closer at the experience of burning out and what we can do to avoid it.

I'm keen to delve into the way we get to brilliance. Before we do that, though, we have to talk about burnout: what it is, why it's so prevalent and how to spot it. Burnout is the opposite to brilliance, but sadly it's the end of the scale that most of us feel closest to in our current climate.

In this chapter, we'll unpack the research on burnout, explore exactly what it is, learn how to spot it and look at strategies to avoid it. We'll look at the difference between stress and burnout, learn why it's not just about workload and explore how to identify our own triggers.

The term 'burnout' was first coined in 1974 by Herbert Freudenberger in his book *Burnout: The High Cost of High Achievement*. He originally defined burnout as 'the extinction of motivation or incentive, especially where one's devotion to a cause or relationship fails to produce the desired results.'

We use 'burnout' to describe physical, mental and emotional exhaustion. Burnout is more than the fatigue we experience at the end of a demanding week, though. It's an exhaustion that doesn't ease up after a long weekend recharging the batteries. It's the kind of tired even sleep can't fix.

According to a 2020 study by the Mental Health Foundation, a quarter of New Zealand adults are struggling with their mental health. The pandemic, and the associated stress, fear and hardships it has brought about, is likely to have exacerbated this. But even before the pandemic, Southern Cross showed a 23.5 per cent rise in stress across businesses in their 2019 study.

In her research on burnout, Christina Maslach, of the University of California, noticed a trend in those she interviewed: workers frequently reported feelings of profound emotional exhaustion, negativity and a crisis in feelings of professional incompetence. From this study Maslach identified six main components of the workplace environment that contribute to burnout:

- workload
- control
- reward
- community
- fairness
- values.

Research suggests that burnout is more common in certain roles, particularly lawyers and GPs, careers associated with long hours and the busy badge of honour. There's also a higher risk of burnout in caring careers such as teaching and nursing. Slightly different to burnout, but with very similar symptoms, is compassion fatigue: the physical, emotional and psychological impact of helping others, often coupled with experiences of stress or trauma. Compassion fatigue can leave those in caring careers more susceptible to burnout: something many of our essential workers have experienced during the COVID-19 outbreak.

Gallup research in 2015 showed that 2.7 million workers in Germany reported feeling the effects of burnout. The Japanese have a word for burnout at its most extreme: *karoshi*, literally meaning death by overwork.

STRESS AND BURNOUT

The World Health Organization predicts that burnout will be a global pandemic in less than a decade, and the World Economic Forum estimates an annual burnout cost of £225 billion to the global economy. We know the organisational cost of burnout is increased turnover, absenteeism and, of course, the obvious impact on performance.

Stress in the workplace is something we've talked about for a long time now, but it's only recently that burnout has become a popular topic of conversation. What's the difference between the two?

I like the distinction *Psychology Today* draws between stress and burnout. It defines burnout as an extended period of stress that feels as though it cannot be ameliorated, and goes on to say if stress is short-lived or tied to a specific goal, it is most likely not harmful. If the stress feels never-ending and comes with feelings of emptiness, apathy and hopelessness, it may be indicative of burnout.

Burnout is more than just being stressed. In fact, a small amount of stress can be motivating for us: it can spur us into action. This type of stress is known as eustress, from the Greek, literally meaning 'good stress'. It is defined as a positive cognitive response to stress that leads to a feeling of fulfilment.

On a continuum of stress we might find boredom on one end and burnout at the other extreme. Eustress is the middle ground we're aiming for.

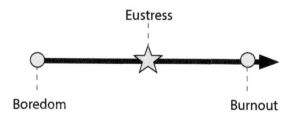

There's an accomplished tired, but then there's the kind of tired where our battery just won't charge and we're constantly running on empty – that's burnout. It's a prolonged stress not fixed by a holiday; a constant exhaustion nothing will shift. It was during my own burnout I came across the saying 'sleep won't help when your soul is tired'.

It's a myth that burnout is just a normal response to long hours or a challenging job. The evidence shows that burnout takes an acute physical toll that cascades well beyond our work.

It's not just exhaustion or stress though – burnout is bigger than that, and so are the consequences. It's the kind of tired that's physically and mentally detrimental to our health. Author of *Thrive* and founder of Huffington Post, Arianna Huffington, has described her own burnout: she was so exhausted she collapsed, hitting her head on her desk, breaking her cheek bone and needing four stitches on her right eye. It's *that* kind of tired.

We tend to correlate burnout to the quantity of our work; to overwork. We're 'doing' too much, we think. However, it can just as easily be the quality of what we're doing that causes stress that leads to burnout. In fact, this is what tires our soul the most. A lack of control, a bullying boss or a toxic work environment. Feeling undermined, or just lacking meaning and purpose in our work.

According to *Psychology Today*; burnout is not simply a result of working long hours or juggling too many tasks, though both these play a role. The cynicism, depression and lethargy that are characteristic of burnout most often occur when a person is not in control of how they carry out their job, or is asked to complete tasks that conflict with their sense of self.

PREVENTING BURNOUT

Now we understand a bit more about burnout, let's talk about how we spot it, what the impacts are and, most importantly, how we can prevent it?

The most common indicators that you're in danger of burning out are exhaustion, a feeling of lack of control, disengagement, trouble focusing, a sense of dread about work and frequent feelings of cynicism or irritability.

The World Health Organization includes burnout in its International Classification of Diseases, noting that sufferers can also experience 'reduced professional efficacy' and energy depletion.

I've summarised the research on burnout into this reference table, which charts burnout's five degrees of seriousness.

1	Loss of energy, feeling too busy to take breaks
2	Overwhelm, lack of focus, working long hours
3	Frustration, lack of results, resentment of others, guilt, anxiety, feelings of not coping, struggle sleeping
4	Feeling of having checked out, discontent, loss of motivation, noncommitment, exhaustion
5	Loss of hope, withdrawal, detachment, illness, depression

I've already told you my burnout story. Comparing my own experience to countless others, I can't help but see recurring themes: feeling like we've failed or not done enough, feeling driven by a need to prove ourselves or to keep up with expectations, fearing being seen as weak or, worse, a failure.

These themes reflect the fact that we tend to hold ourselves to an impossible standard. Then we feel shame for not being able to deliver. In my experience, it's not poor performers who burn out.

We don't burn out because we're not capable – in fact, the opposite is true. The more capable we are, the more likely we are to burn out. It's the drive of the high achiever that leads us down this path.

We're also more likely to be given more responsibilities and more work when we're good at what we do. There's an old saying 'if you want something done, give it to someone who is busy'. This can be the high achiever's curse. Because we take on a lot and make sure we over-deliver, we're more likely to attract more work.

High achievers are given more work because of their competence and track record, which puts them at higher risk of overworking, having too much on their plate and ultimately burning out.

And, of course, we can't say no, for fear of not being seen as up to the job, for fear of looking weak or for fear of being seen as not coping. Our cultures and societal norms in this regard keep us pushing until we hit a wall; we say yes until we collapse under the weight of all the commitments we've made – then we feel like a failure.

If this resonates, remember: we've been set up to fail. We can't perform at our peak in this kind of environment, no matter how good we are.

Where burnout is concerned, the recurring themes revolve around our need to over-deliver. This either comes from a belief that going the extra mile will lead to success, promotion or achievement, or from a feeling of lack. If we don't have confidence in our abilities, or feel like we're in a job that's too big for us, we're going to work twice as hard in a bid to overcome these feelings of doubt. We want to prove ourselves and to ensure we don't get 'found out'.

If we're tired, burned out and not at our best, everything else drops on the gauge too; not just our energy. This decreases our resilience, our confidence and our ability to focus. It affects our tolerance levels towards those we love, our ability to bounce back from setbacks and our capacity to make decisions and come up with great ideas.

In this situation, our cognitive function declines, disrupting our creativity and our problem-solving abilities and lowering our emotional intelligence. Being in this state also negatively impacts our memory, concentration and attention – and just about everything we need to be good at our work. These are the skills we lose when we're burned out, and they are also the skills critical to great leadership. All of this impact comes from a suboptimal, tired mind and, of course, the worse that gets the bigger the impact. Not a great recipe for peak performance.

It can be a vicious cycle, especially where confidence is concerned. We know burnout erodes self-belief and confidence, but it's also worth noting that lack of confidence and self-belief can also drive overwork and lead to burnout. We over-deliver in a bid to prove we're better than we actually feel we are.

KNOWING YOUR TRIGGERS

So how do we avoid burnout? What triggers should we look out for?

Well, if you're tired all the time, despite getting plenty of sleep; if you're constantly fighting off coughs and colds – always being on the verge of sickness; if you're struggling to motivate yourself, and not finding joy in the things you used to love or don't have the motivation to do these things … you're on notice burnout is close.

In this state, we become less tolerant of those around us. We reach for the wrong food or increase our alcohol intake as a coping mechanism. When we're exhausted, we tend to choose TV over exercise, or takeaways over cooking, or we skip meals completely because of a loss of appetite – these are all potential burnout signs.

And, of course, the most obvious sign is when we truly hit burnout, and end up in bed, completely devoid of energy and interest in life. This was certainly my experience – but we're all different.

How do we take what we know and apply it to our own experience?

Most of us know what it's like to be at our best; we've been there before. Likewise, we know what it's like when we're about to hit a wall and get sick: when we've overdone it, left it too late or burned the candle at both ends.

I like to think of this in terms of a traffic light. We all have green and red zones, and they look different for us all.

The red light stops us completely; it's our ground zero. The green light is when we're all go and at our best. The amber light, in between, is important: it's our warning system. When we slip from green, before we hit red, the amber light gives us an opportunity to act and pre-empt hitting the wall and slipping into that red zone: burnout.

For me, that amber light is a twitch in the corner of my eye, a sore throat and a constant tiredness. It's noticing I'm less tolerant and a bit snappy with loved ones. This is my amber light; my warning to back off, take a rest and pre-empt the approaching red zone.

Another way to think about this is in terms of the petrol warning light in the car. When you know your tank is nearing empty, stop and refuel, to avoid being left on the side of the road.

EXERCISE

So what do these traffic lights look like for you? What do you notice about yourself when you're at your best, on green? What about when you're at your worst and close to burnout, on red? And what about that bit in between: what are the early warning signs you get at the amber light?

See if you can articulate what each of the three looks like for you:

	When I'm in the green zone I
	When I'm in the amber zone I
	When I'm in the red zone I

USEFUL STRATEGIES

There's no shame in hitting red. We've all been there, or close to it. It's not the sign of failure we so often feel it is, and there is always a way back.

In my experience, when we hit rock bottom there's only one

way up. It can be through our greatest challenges that we get a glimpse of our true gifts. Looking back, my burnout was a turning point for me in many ways. It forced me to change everything about my life and led to the work I'm doing now.

The silver lining for those who end up burning out is that sometimes a breakdown can lead to a breakthrough. Burnout is the loudest message our body can give us when it gives up. It leaves us no option but to change things.

So once we've been in the red, how do we make sure it doesn't happen again?

We've talked about the importance of rest, breaks, balance and self-care, and we'll expand on those ideas in the next chapter. These concepts are often easier understood than done. I don't know about you, but I struggle to say no. I always want to help people out, take on more, bite off more than I can chew. I struggle to leave enough time for myself. It can leave my schedule too full, and when my schedule gets out of hand, time for myself is hard to find.

Last year, I set up automatic scheduling for all of my appointments. It links directly to my diary and provides a link people can use to book available space for calls and meetings without ever having to talk to me. This has been great for saving time, but I also noticed that, at first, it meant I'd end up with far too many bookings, and struggle to fit in the stuff I needed to do for me as well. On reflection, the freedom to find time for myself had been one of the reasons I chose to work for myself. I'd seemingly given it away to an online scheduling tool!

Then, I discovered that my scheduling tool has a buffer setting. This is a time limit you can set between meetings, to give you time to breathe.

So often, we find ourselves in back-to-back meetings, without time to eat away from our desk or even go to the bathroom. But to be our best, we need time between meetings to collect our thoughts, prepare and take a breath – or at least a transition.

Do you have a buffer? How can you create one?

Your buffer might not be via an electronic scheduling tool – but the principle is the same. How can you create space in your schedule for *you*: time to breathe and time for an effective transition between activities?

Before so much of our lives came to be conducted online, our buffers used to come in the form of travel between meetings. These days, the amount of time we spend on Zoom or working from home mean that the buffers are disappearing.

Although I've handed control of my diary to an online scheduling tool, I have managed to do it in a way that restored my ability to keep some time for myself. I've also blocked out one day a week in my diary that's solely for me – whether that's to catch up on admin or to get to the beach. It gives me some breathing space, and some flexibility in the busy weeks. I also know now that there's one less excuse to find time for the things that keep me effective, help my wellness and are essential to keeping me at my best.

Think about how you can keep some time up your sleeve for yourself between the appointments you've committed to in your diary: some breathing space.

Buffers can also come in the form of support: things or people we can lean on.

I'm reminded of this when I'm around the port and I'm watching the container ships come in.

One particular winter day, I was watching boats come into Wellington Harbour. As the swell whipped around the harbour and the rain and wind blasted the window, I watched a tiny tugboat head off to bring a container ship in.

Those ships are massive: they sail from the other side of the world in the open ocean, withstanding conditions I can only imagine. Yet when they get to port, they need to wait for these tiny little tugboats to come and guide them in.

I think this sums up our need for support. Sometimes the swell is heavy; sometimes the storms set in. Like the container ships, we're all capable of withstanding the weather – but sometimes we need a tugboat to bring us home. Sometimes we encounter tricky patches we're not used to or haven't navigated before, and in these situations we need support.

Our support tugboats can be in the form of people, learnings, knowledge or reflection. Support can also come in the form of the things we do – yoga and meditation have so often been my tugboats, guiding me safely to port.

Watching these tiny tugs also makes me realise that it's often the small things in life that really make a big difference. Even the big strong container ships need support to navigate the tricky bits. So do we.

So who, or what, is *your* tugboat in the storm?

As we consider taking back control of our schedules, and how we can get the support we need, we should also look at how we can achieve more balance. In the next chapter, we'll delve into self-care and building resilience to stave off burnout. This is the foundation from which we build our brilliance.

TOP TIPS FOR AVOIDING BURNOUT:

- Mind your busyness.
- Get support.
- Regain control of your schedule.
- Take time for you – rest, recharge and relax.
- Invest in self-care.
- Reprioritise what matters and learn to say no.
- Know your triggers.
- Prioritise quality over quantity.

SUSTAINABLE BRILLIANCE

Now we understand burnout and have some strategies to manage it, how do we ensure ongoing performance and sustainability?

In this chapter we'll uncover the secrets to building resilience and sustaining our energy in a way that means we're better equipped to avoid burnout. Resilience is the energy that allows us to shine, and therefore powers brilliance.

It's important and appropriate here to discuss the expectations we place on ourselves and how to ensure we're not dimming our light. We need to make sure we're approaching this realistically, without setting the bar at an unrealistic height. We'll look at what it is that gives you energy, and what happens during the tough times. Looking particularly at our recent pandemic, we'll explore the impacts this has had, what the research tells us and what is *actually* normal in our new normal.

Building resilience is key to giving us the energy we need to perform. We do this by investing in self-care. When we're effectively caring for ourselves, we're sustainable, and at less risk of burning out.

Sustainability is a popular word in business these days – but how often do we apply it to ourselves? The prevalence of burnout and the way we approach our work in our society would suggest we've not placed enough attention on ensuring we, ourselves, are a sustainable resource. After all, our energy is the most significant resource we have as individuals. It's a predetermining factor in peak performance. We know that, without it, we get sick.

For me, sustainability is resilience. It's our energy to be our best and our ability to bounce back from the tough times. I believe building resilience is the best way to ensure we're sustainable, as well as forming sensible habits in terms of work–life balance: how we use our time.

Resilient people can motivate themselves in the face of setbacks. They are optimistic; they learn from their mistakes, solve problems and look for solutions. They have self-control and they are not afraid to seek assistance from others.

Things don't always go to plan; we have to deal with challenging situations or people. Resilient people perform better, and are healthier and happier. That's why building resilience is a key aspect of peak performance.

If you've heard me talk about this, you'll know I'm an advocate for resilience being a constant focus: not just something we wish for when we need it. It's too late at that point. I liken it to a bank account we pay into over time: we can withdraw funds when we need them, when the tough times hit.

It's easy to be happy when everything is going well, but we know that's not always the case, and that's why we should all have a focus on building our resilience and looking after ourselves. Tough times come to us all at some point. We can't always control the things that happen to us, but we can control how we react to them, and a massive determining factor in this respect is our resilience.

The COVID-19 outbreak has been a true test of this: we've all struggled to change our jobs, our working patterns and our workload, amid the uncertainty a global pandemic brings.

A tree grows its roots when the weather is fine so that, when the storms come, it stays standing strong. If we wait until we need resilience to start building it, we'll find we're trying to grow roots in the midst of a storm.

We spend a lot of our time trying to avoid the bad things in life while simultaneously chasing after the good. We cling on when we get something good, hoping it'll never leave – yet in reality, both good and bad will always come and go.

Regardless of who we work for and what job we have, we will come across people who frustrate us, people who underperform and people who think and act differently to us. We'll also likely be involved in restructures or even redundancies, and have to leave a job or adapt to a change that wasn't our own choice.

The saying is true: we can't always control what happens to us, but we can control how we react to it. Buddhists have a great analogy for this, which perfectly sums up how our attitude and mindset affect our resilience: the second arrow analogy.

If we're walking through the forest and we get hit by an arrow, we have a problem, and it causes us pain. Our reaction to this problem is like being hit by a second arrow in the same place. Now we have two problems and double the pain: but the second arrow is one that we shot ourselves.

What's important is not so much what happens to us, but how we react to it. We tend to get upset and angry about the initial problem. Maybe our car has broken down: that is the first arrow, and the resulting pain is not of our doing. If we choose to get angry and upset about this, that's the second arrow. It will double our pain but do little to resolve the first problem – and we shot that arrow ourselves.

One of the tools I use in my workshops is Stephen Covey's circles of influence concept. It really helps cut through our concerns to empower us to take action.

We all have a wide range of concerns in our life: things we care about that affect us but that we have little or no control over.

Some of these concerns we can influence; some of them we can't.

We have a choice about what we choose to spend our time and energy on. If we focus on all of our concerns and worries, we might find they get bigger with the attention we give them, but we won't be able to take any significant action to mitigate them, then we'll get depressed and nothing much will change. This leads to blame and feelings of victimisation.

Concerns over things we can't control belong in Covey's outer circle: things like the stock market, war, pandemics, government policy or traffic jams.

When we focus on the things we *can* influence – Covey's inner circle – we become more proactive. Focusing on this inner circle means our efforts make a more positive difference to our results.

This can be as simple as our reaction to something or aspects of bigger problems we can take action on. It doesn't mean direct control; for example, we might not be able to stop climate change, but we can focus on our own behaviour and what we do around our home to help contribute in this space.

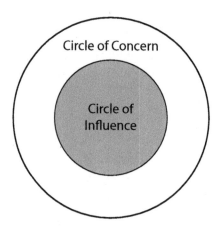

When we focus our energy in our circle of influence, it enlarges the inner circle and therefore our influence. It's liberating to know we can make a difference and control even small aspects of our concerns.

As an example: if the business we work for is closing and we're being made redundant, there's nothing we can do about that; it sits in the outer circle. In this case, focusing on the inner circle might look like updating our CV, seeking outplacement support or talking to a friend who mentioned last week their company might be looking for new staff.

The aim is for our focus to be on those things we can control or influence, and away from the things we have no control over. Don't waste energy on things you can't do anything about.

As the Dalai Lama puts it, 'If there is a solution to the problem, then we don't need to worry. If there isn't a solution to the problem, then there's no point worrying.'

Take a look at the circle diagram above and consider some of your own concerns.

- Which circle are you spending most of your time and energy in?

- What are some of your current concerns? Which circle do they fit in? What can you do about the ones that fall in the inner circle?

IT'S OK NOT TO BE OK

What about the really bad times, though? The times where we feel like there's no hope – where we can't see a light at the end of the tunnel? As much as I'm an advocate for a solutions-focused positive outlook during our tough times, I also acknowledge that, sometimes, we're simply at the end of the line. This can be especially true for those experiencing burnout, loss, depression or severe illness.

Sometimes we hit a wall, and when that happens we must acknowledge it, and understand its place in the burnout to brilliance journey.

Just because we're *capable* of brilliance doesn't mean we'll hit that height all the time. In fact, some days, even if we're not at the end of the line I'm talking about, we'll simply not be at our best – and that's also a normal part of being human. Even gold medal-winning Olympians struggle to hit the dizzy heights of the world's expectations.

Our culture is to expect the best, and assume everything is fine, to the point we're uncomfortable with the truth when it's not. When we suspect someone might be struggling, we don't know what to do or say – we don't wish to make others uncomfortable by admitting the truth. There's a stigma that comes with admitting we're not ok.

Our standard answer to 'How are you?' tends to be 'Yeah, good, fine, thanks.' Or words to that effect – regardless of what's actually happening in our life.

To be honest, even the person asking the question 'how are you?' is expecting this standard response – they probably don't want to hear 'My dog has died, I've got too much work on and my marriage is at breaking point' as a response, even if it's the truth.

We don't like to share when things are going wrong, and we don't always feel we have 'permission' to be sad. We feel like we must always put on a brave face: to be coping, to be the optimist, to be the strong one. When we do feel sad, we often reach for distractions to bury those feelings.

These days, we feel like we can't allow ourselves to be upset.

We chase the good and avoid the bad in life – but both come and go, and sometimes the best thing to do is acknowledge this, sit with it and allow it to pass.

Last year, my wife and I had a miscarriage. Afterwards, life seemed to get tough, and I was feeling low. Physically, my menstrual cycle was all over the place and worsening my mood, so I went to the doctor. I was hoping for a fix – something to stop the pain – but the response she gave me was, 'This is normal. After what you've been through, it's normal to feel sad, and sometimes that affects us physically.'

It was the first time I'd thought of my feelings of sadness as normal and something we all experience in tough times, rather than an intrusion on my happiness and something that needed to be 'fixed'.

Sometimes it's ok not to be ok. It's easy to be happy when things are going well, but what about the difficult times? If we only allow ourselves to be happy when things are perfect, we'll be waiting for happiness a long time.

How do we still cultivate happiness when times are tough?

Many happy people have grown from their darkest times and are products of the experiences they've learned from. Sometimes the fact is that they have lost everything in order to gain their current happiness. 'It's through the cracks the light gets in,' as the saying goes.

One of the most important questions we can ask is 'Are you ok?' Not just to others, but also ourselves.

This is especially true in recent times: our mental health has been tested like never before, on a global scale, during the pandemic.

Many of us struggled during the lockdowns and the uncertainty that came with the outbreak. To be honest, that was the normal response, in these circumstances.

Whether it was being apart from loved ones, illness, fear, the struggle with kids, home schooling, job security worries or the prospect of getting COVID – there was a lot to feel upset about.

More specifically, COVID has meant that many of us have missed big family events like births and deaths (in the case of deaths, in particular, some of us have been unable to grieve as we usually do, gain closure or visit loved ones in hospital). Some of us have lost our businesses overnight, and have been wondering how we'll pay the bills. Some of us will have tested positive for COVID and realised we've passed it to our family. *Most* of us have lost all our usual mental health supports: people, places, activities or freedoms. Every bit of the pandemic has been a test on our already stretched mental health.

Everything becomes harder in circumstances like this: meal planning, supermarket shopping or just waking up and getting on with the day. We're more distracted than normal: more anxious, less motivated and certainly less innovative. We struggle with the guilt that comes with not being able to be at our best and perform in the way we know we can.

Whilst battling the pandemic, home schooling the kids and trying to work from the kitchen table, it's not surprising our performance may have dipped. We also might find we're less able to achieve or 'prove ourselves' from the home office like we can in the workplace. All of this can lead to productivity guilt. We feel guilty if we're working all day and the kids feel abandoned. Or we feel guilty if we stopped work at 3 pm to spend time with the kids. And then, on top of all this, we feel guilty we're not training for a marathon in our spare time, or doing personal development webinars, or baking bread.

Nothing about our pandemic climate has been normal. If you have struggled or haven't been performing at your peak, that's ok. In fact, that's probably the most normal part of the whole situation.

It's ok not to be ok: especially in times like these.

THE IMPORTANCE OF SELF-CARE

'Almost everything will work again if you unplug it for a few
minutes, including you.' – Anne Lamott

One of the best ways we can prepare ourselves for tough times and
help ourselves work through them is to invest in ourselves: to take
what we need, seek support and put ourselves first. I am of course
talking about self-care: Not in an 'Instagram opportunity' way but
in a prioritising our health and recharging our batteries kind of way.

Whether it's sitting with a cup of tea first thing in the morning
before anyone else is up, or going to bed early to read – find space
in your life to take time out.

If we *don't* take this time out for ourselves, the effect will be
something like when our phone battery dies before we can get to the
charger: we've overused it, and not given the batteries time to refill.

I use self-care as the foundation from which I build. If I feel
good and have plenty of energy, everything else seems so much
easier, even when the tough times hit.

Self-care is a critical part of not only building our resilience but
also giving us the mental clarity to create and the energy to succeed.

As a solopreneur, I see self-care as part of my job. If I go down,
my whole business does.

I love a massage once a month, it's a non negotiable not a luxury
item for me. I see it as part of preparing for my work, like the All
Blacks and Olympians you see getting massages before and after
games. It's not for pleasure but so they can perform. I view this as
the same for me just with a lot less running!

Self-care is not in any of our job descriptions, but I think it
should be. Maybe then we'd take it more seriously? Or at least we'd
feel like we had permission to prioritise it, in the same way we do

our workload. If you're a leader, in particular, it's your job to be at your best, to manage your energy and know what you need. You'll only be capable of leading others if you first lead yourself.

When the most successful people in our society let us into their performance secrets, they often talk about their morning routines, their self-care, how they centre themselves. I believe this is the key to success and how we can all reach our potential, because I've seen the difference it's made for me.

Self-care looks different for everyone. It doesn't have to cost money, take lots of time or be difficult. In fact, it should be the opposite – it should make life easier.

What do you do for your self-care? Is it enough? When do you do it, and how do you make the time for it?

Here are a few ideas for self-care:

- morning meditation
- a walk in nature
- yoga stretches
- exercise or sport
- nutrition
- adequate sleep
- gratitude
- deep breaths
- putting fresh sheets on the bed
- lighting your favourite candle
- playing your favourite song
- calling your best friend
- having a bath

- watching a funny movie
- learning something new
- a swim
- taking time away from technology
- journaling.

Pick one thing that's achievable and works for you, and focus on making that a priority in your day. Consider what you can factor into the things you're already doing. For example, you could play your favourite song on the way to work, or do a meditation via an app whilst you're on the bus. Take your lunch break outside, sitting under a tree. In this way, you'll be fitting healthy self-care habits into things you're doing anyway.

Some quick wins and great starting points for self-care include the food we eat, how much we move and our sleep.

It's easy to think going to bed early wastes time that could be spent doing other things, but personally I find that being fresh and rested saves me time. Not being tired during the day helps me function better; when I've slept well, tasks don't take as long, I focus more, my mind is sharp, I solve problems quicker and the day flows better. This is an investment in time.

Feeling healthy and full of energy helps me cope with what life throws at me: I'm more inclined to be optimistic, have positive interactions with others (even those who may irritate me) and feel good about myself when I'm not tired and run down. My self-talk is healthier, and I'm less hard on myself – another aspect of self-care.

I don't mind admitting I'm in bed most nights before 10 pm. It means I wake up fresh and ready for the day ahead. I spent years dragging myself out of bed in the mornings; I was desperately attached to the snooze button. As a result, I'd feel sluggish most of the morning, and it'd take a few cups of caffeine to lift the brain fog.

These days, I find my morning routine is vital to starting the day well. With my new morning routine, my brain functions better, and my mind is clearer and therefore more creative.

These days, my mornings look like this: I get up early, do some stretches and sit for 10 minutes to meditate (sometimes longer if I've got the time, and sometimes not at all. I believe in the 80:20 rule: if we're doing things 80 per cent of the time, the 20 per cent we miss is inconsequential). I then have breakfast and get ready for the day. Some mornings, I get outside, too, and walk the dog before I start work.

It's the small, simple things that make the difference: the things that don't cost money or take up too much extra time, because, let's face it, we need self-care because we're so short on time.

Those who know me know I'm a fan of the sauna, particularly in the winter. It's a warm, quiet, dark space, and I feel instantly relaxed when I'm in there. It's also where a lot of my thinking happens, so it gives me important processing time.

Self-care is about having time to ourselves where we can just *be* and relax – it doesn't necessarily have to be in a sauna!

Where do you find thinking space? This space is essential for our creativity and innovation; we can't access those qualities in our brain when we're constantly busy and stuck in 'doing' mode. Being in the sauna staring at the ceiling may not sound like me at my most productive – in fact, it might sound like I'm doing nothing – and yet the sauna is often where I have my best ideas.

Like everyone, I find self-care hard. I'm less motivated to do the things I know help when I need them the most, and I experience guilt and shame when I don't live up to my own high expectations. This brings me to my next point.

THE SELF-CARE SHAME HOLE

It's only fair that I point out that my own self-care plan has varying degrees of success. I'm not doing all of my self-care strategies all of the time – and sometimes I'm doing none of it and I'm busy beating myself up and sitting in my shame hole eating carbs!

No one is perfect, despite what Instagram feeds may suggest. If we have a plan of self-care activities to pick from, though, and we know what works for us, we're more likely to be able to fill the tank before it runs empty.

Self-care has become a bit of a buzz word, and for many (including me), another stick to beat ourselves with. Prior to my burnout I was an all-or-nothing personality, which means I'm either doing a juice detox or eating chips and sinking wine; training for a 10-kilometre run or lying on the couch. I didn't just learn to meditate – I went to live with Buddhists. When I first came across Wim Hof (the godfather of cold therapy), I didn't just want to do a few cold showers; I decided I'd do year-round sea swimming in Wellington every day! Needless to say, that lasted about a day: I hate the cold. Then I felt like a failure.

It'll come as no surprise that, when I first discovered the importance of self-care, I wanted to do it all. I treated it like another to-do list that I had to achieve, and as a result I was always falling short.

I'd beat myself up for having a burger at the weekend, because everyone on Instagram seemed to be blogging about fasting. I'd feel like a failure if I'd only made it to yoga once this week, because everyone on Instagram seemed to be doing an hour in their garden each day at 6 am, decked out in lululemon.

My perception of how others achieved self-care, and of what I expected a 'good, healthy person' to do, were so unrealistic – and yet I used that perception as the marker of my own success. No wonder my results were less than perfect most of the time!

In those days, my self-care plan would often look like this:

Expectation: Rise at 5 am, meditate, do yoga, go for a sea swim, make a juice for breakfast, write in my gratitude journal and walk the dog.

Reality: Sleep in until 7.30 am, make three cups of tea and drink them in bed, surf social media, eat toast and get up to put the bins out. Feel like a failure, let the dog out.

Social media – especially Instagram – has increased the guilt trip for many of us. Wellness warriors fill their feeds with perfect bodies and updates about all the juices they are drinking and yoga they are doing. We forget that, for these people, social media itself is a full-time job, and we wonder why we can't repeat their success in our own busy lives, alongside our own full-time jobs. We tell ourselves we're lazy, useless, not good enough and failing at self-care – the guilt trip begins.

Self-care is supposed to make us feel better and improve our health, but in this Instagram age we're using it as a stick to beat ourselves with. I used to find that when I woke up on a Sunday after a few glasses of wine the night before, I'd feel bad. I'd tell myself 'it serves you right; you shouldn't be drinking. It's bad for you; you should be more like those sober wellness warriors on Instagram. You deserve to feel bad; maybe this will help you stop.'

Then I'd disappear down a shame hole with a packet of chips to comfort me. It wasn't so much the wine that made me feel bad; it was the guilt trip I'd sent myself on.

We are in danger of setting ourselves up to fail when we compare our own habits with an Instagram lifestyle that's simply not achievable. We tell ourselves that we're a bad person if we eat cake or have a few drinks – that if we lie on the couch instead of going to the gym one night, we're lazy and useless. Moderation is the key, and the 80:20 rule should apply. Sometimes the best thing we can do for our self-care is to let go of perfection and give ourselves a break. Not everyone is three years sober, living on celery and doing two hours of yoga every day.

Ask yourself where the middle ground is. What's reasonable, and what's better than nothing? I might not fancy the gym, but a walk around the block might seem doable, and at least make me feel like I've moved today.

Moderation is a struggle for those of us who are all-or-nothing types. These excessively high bars we set ourselves are common for high achievers. I had a client recently tell me she'd failed at her wellness goals this week. When I asked her to explain, she told me, 'I only went to the gym three times; I did yoga once and I missed three days on the meditation app.' I reflected this back to her from the other angle: 'Look at what you *did* do; not what you didn't.' Both of us could then see she'd achieved her goal of improving her self-care – she was beating herself up for not meeting her unrealistic expectations of perfection.

I'm a big believer in the power of tiny gains: it's the small things that make the biggest difference. James Clear explains this beautifully in his book *Atomic Habits*, which we'll talk about later. His 1 percent improvement methodology has stuck with me. It helps break big goals like 'I need to be healthier' down into more manageable actions. 'I'll just walk around the block at lunchtime today' might be a great start.

These days, instead of trying to do all the things on my self-care list and recreate the life of an Instagram wellness warrior, I pick one thing. I ask myself 'what's the focus today?' It might be work-related, if my to-do list is overflowing or there's a looming deadline. On those days, if I don't do any exercise, I'm not going to beat myself up. Or it might be that today's focus is self-care, because I've had a busy week. On those days, if my day centres on a walk along the beach and some yoga stretches, I can say it's a successful day despite not getting through the to-do list. I pick my one thing as the day's focus and tend to do that first. Then, not only do I have a sense of achievement, but anything I do from that point is a bonus. It's so much more achievable – and the beauty is that every day is another chance to pick a different focus or to address something I let slide yesterday.

I love the saying 'the grass is always greener where you water it', and I use it to stop comparing myself to others, which is an easy trap to fall into and a great way to send us on the guilt-and-shame trip. When I'm focusing on the things I'm doing and feeling a sense of achievement for tiny progress steps, I'm less likely to compare myself to others, who I tend to assume are doing more – even though I don't really know that. For all I know, *they're* looking at *my* social media thinking I'm the very wellness warrior they're trying to emulate.

I was recently in one of New Zealand's managed isolation and quarantine (MIQ) facilities – part of New Zealand's response to the COVID-19 threat, for travellers returning to New Zealand. While I was in the MIQ hotel, I took great delight in seeing what everyone else had ordered for dinner as I walked down the corridor for my daily outdoor time. Peering into the empty bags, I thought to myself 'wow; I'm actually quite healthy; most of these people are living on Coke and KFC'. And yet I'd been telling myself I needed to get into shape, and should be hiring a spin bike for the room and running 100 laps of the car park, like others I'd seen on Facebook – even though I hate spin.

We tend to focus on the bits we miss or the things we're *not* doing; this can be at the expense of celebrating what we are doing well. Self-care can be small steps, and it only needs to be one thing. It's not about doing all of the self-care activities every day; it's about picking one thing and not putting the pressure on ourselves to be perfect. We're all human, and a 'lapse' can be ok. In, fact allowing for lapses can be critical for our self-care: it's not always the lapse that affects us as much as the way we beat ourselves up about it.

THE PANDEMIC EFFECT

All of this is particularly true in the tough times. Times of uncertainty and change are much more challenging. No situation has taught us this more truly than the COVID-19 pandemic and associated lockdowns.

The 'new normal' isn't really normal at all. What *is* normal is to struggle during times like these. Since the appearance of COVID-19, I've noticed that I eat more, and I tend to walk around in my PJs more; dressing for a meeting somehow became putting a bra and shirt over the bottom half of my PJs so I was camera ready. I'd never dream of this in normal circumstances – but these *aren't* normal circumstances; I think we all need special dispensation.

Given most of us have struggled at some point during the pandemic, now is not the time to be beating ourselves up for not being perfect.

Despite this, there's been a pressure, during lockdown, to spend more time baking or exercising or doing all those online courses we signed up for – whilst balancing home schooling, working from home and the general stress and anxiety that comes from periods of uncertainty and change.

It's not surprising that COVID-19 has had an impact on our energy, our resilience and, ultimately, our brilliance. Striving for brilliance at times like these is like trying to shine a light during a power cut. It's become commonplace for high achievers to experience productivity guilt recently; we're not as motivated about our work as we used to be.

It's normal, during a pandemic, for us to not be at our best and to indulge in habits we know aren't necessarily healthy. The way I see it, these habits are a temporary fix – a bridge to get us out of the hole we find ourselves in. We should expect to be less tolerant and less motivated when our freedoms have been removed overnight.

I'm the most optimistic, hopeful person I know – and yet I'm not ok during times like this. I think that's normal. It reminds me of a line from the movie *Bohemian Rhapsody*, about Freddie Mercury: 'being human is a condition that requires a little anaesthesia'. Whilst I'm not promoting the idea that we should eat and drink ourselves to excess, I understand why we might be tempted to take the edge off, to seek to numb out some of the uncomfortable moments these big challenges bring.

The quote from *Bohemian Rhapsody* rang particularly true for me during New Zealand's second pandemic lockdown, which coincided with me moving house, relocating cities and travelling back to the UK to see family.

If comfort eating was an Olympic sport, I'd fancy myself to win gold. I've reverted to food for comfort for as long as I can remember – so was it realistic to expect myself to diet during the pandemic? And if not (because of course not) does that make me less brilliant? I can still shine with a couple of extra pandemic kilos attached – and diet when times are less challenging.

My scrolling and device time whilst I was in MIQ went up 300 per cent, according to my app. Did I beat myself up or feel like a failure because of that? Not like I would normally – because these weren't normal circumstances. I allowed myself two weeks off my normal rules – let's face it, being in MIQ was hard enough. I wanted to go easy on myself, and recognise the unique situation I was in and what was possible given the parameters. Contact with the outside world became more important, as did comparing what I'd had for dinner with others in quarantine facilities across the city.

When it comes to the pandemic, it's important to remember we're not alone. More than 40 percent of adults in England gained weight during the pandemic, a survey suggests: the average gain was just over 3 kilograms. Public Health England surveyed 5,000 people and discovered COVID lockdowns and disrupted daily routines have made it challenging for people to eat healthily and keep fit.

Snacking and comfort eating were given as the main contributor by about half of those who said they'd gained weight.

According to Alcohol Healthwatch data from the first national lockdown in New Zealand, almost 20 per cent of New Zealanders increased their alcohol consumption during that time.

I think it's important we have this conversation, so we can get some perspective around our crazy expectations: to see what's normal and to know that, if we're struggling, it's not just us. Again, I think moderation is the key. There can be a fine line between giving ourselves a break during tough times and using the tough times as a springboard for things to get out of hand. If you feel like your health is at risk because of the bad habits you've picked up over the course of the pandemic, seek help and support to get you back on track. We know that, left unchecked, bad habits can be come detrimental to our health. Find your middle ground. Don't use bad habits as a stick to beat yourself with, but also know when enough is enough. We'll talk more about habits shortly.

As I write this, the country is emerging from another lockdown, and it is spring. Flowers are blooming and buds are bursting. I'm not a gardener, but my wife is. I always wonder at the resilience of the plants when I see her cut them back to nothing but stumps. I wonder how these twigs will survive – yet each spring green shoots appear and they grow back stronger than ever. We can be like that too. Sometimes, being curtailed or cut back gives us the chance to grow back stronger. Like the buds bursting forth in spring we too can use these times of dormancy and renewal to come back better than ever.

THINGS WE DON'T DO

We've talked about the basics that keep us well, and about setting realistic expectations, but self-care extends far beyond what we do.

Self-care is also about how we allow ourselves to be treated: the people we hang out with, how we allow others to treat us, the voice inside our head, the food we put into our body, the way we feel when we look in the mirror, how busy we allow ourselves to be, and whether we care enough about ourselves to make time for ourselves.

Self-care is also as much about what we *don't* do as what we do. It's about setting good boundaries and saying no as well as delegating. This is critical in ensuring we can perform, and it's something we can struggle with if we're driven to achieve.

When we take time to focus on self-care, everyone around us benefits too. If we're compassionate by nature, we can find we're last on our own list – but how can we give to others if we're pouring from an empty cup?

Taking a break from technology once a month for a day or two helps clear my mind and gives me a break from the constant social media messaging and resulting comparisons: the not-good-enough spiral it's easy to get caught up in – this is an act of self-care.

Often when I wake up, I spend a few minutes simply sitting in silence before the rest of the house wakes – this is also an act of self-care.

Choosing who my friends are, the people I work with and the work I do each day also contributes to my self-care.

Who we choose to hang around with, the office gossip we engage in and the way we let our bosses treat us also count as self-care measures – they will either add to or detract from our resilience and our ability to perform.

Leaving a company that doesn't align to our values, a boss who mistreats us or a partner who doesn't respect us – these are all acts of self-care. Self-care is also saying no to additional demands when we're overscheduled.

It can be a very hard thing to do, saying no. It's too easy to feel like in saying no we're letting people down. I now treat saying no as a way of protecting myself and ensuring I stay in top form, able to deliver on expectations and be good to others.

Saying no to that one extra meeting when the week is full means I've more energy when I get home to be with my family. Saying no to another 6 am start because I've had 6 am starts all week means that, when I get on stage, people get the whole me, not a 60 per cent tired version.

'No' doesn't have to be an absolute negative or a sign I don't care, I can't deliver or I'm willing to let people down. 'No' can take many forms; for example:

- 'Not right now. Maybe when I'm less busy.'

- 'No, but thanks for asking. I really appreciate you thinking of me.'

- 'No, but I might know someone else who can help.'

- 'No, not this time, but feel free to ask next time.'

- 'No, but I'd have loved to if I had the time.'

- 'No, because I'm doing x, y and z instead.'

- 'I already have plans' or 'Something else has come up.'

- 'I'm not available, but let's reschedule.'

Next time you're overscheduled, remember to see balancing the busyness as an act of self-care.

Next time you're in an uneven relationship or a negative conversation, remember to see removing yourself as an act of self-care. Next time you have to say no, remember to see it as looking after yourself, allowing you to give more to others, and deliver on your own expectations.

We perform best when we're rested, refreshed and not stressed.

We need to start seeing self-care and time out as a must-have – a priority in terms of our resilience, not a nice-to-have saved for when we've got time.

Self-care is our foundation: it's where everything else builds from, and it's how we refuel our tank and sustain the energy to be our best. Self-care is made up of the small things, and because they're the small things we can easily overlook them – but they make such a big difference.

FILLING YOUR CUP

If burnout is energy depletion, then self-care is refuelling the tank. It's charging the batteries that exist within us: the batteries that control our brilliance.

When we're in our red zone and burning out, recharging can feel like filling a bucket with a hole in it: as fast as we try to fill it up it's still close to empty.

One of the things that refuels me is being out in nature and feeling the sun on my skin – to the point at which I think I may have been a lizard in a former life. I can literally feel the battery markers lighting up as I bask on a rock!

You've probably heard the popular saying 'you can't pour from an empty cup'. A full cup leads to a happy life, a charged battery and of course more energy. Have you thought about what fills or drains *your* cup?

I know yoga, meditation, the beach and nutritious food fill my cup, as does getting out and meeting people and making a difference through my work. I also know that, as an introvert, too much socialising leaves my cup needing a refill by way of solitude and reflection time. My family cup was left half empty during the first stage of the pandemic, when I couldn't visit loved ones overseas.

My cup used to contain a lot of things I thought would make me happy or things I thought I should be doing. As a result, I was very busy, but really my cup was empty not full. Life was overflowing with things to do but it left me feeling drained and empty. There is a difference between full and fulfilled; this is important to remember where our cups are concerned.

The table below gives some examples of things that fill, and drain, my own cup. Over the page there's a table I've left blank for you to complete your own audit and contemplate what fills and drains your cup.

WHAT FILLS MY CUP	WHAT DRAINS MY CUP
Quality time with my wife	Busyness
Meditation	Scrolling on social media
Going for a beach walk	Not doing enough exercise
Holidays	Eating too much sugar or
Dog cuddles	takeaways
Surfing	Too many wines
Yoga	Too many social events
Solitude and reflection	Not getting out in nature
	Not getting enough sleep

Burnout to Brilliance

WHAT FILLS YOUR CUP	WHAT DRAINS YOUR CUP

IS WORK-LIFE BALANCE REALLY A THING?

Whilst we're on the subject of self-care, and managing our energy and balance, let's talk about work-life balance.

For so long in our culture, it seems, we've talked about the quest for work-life balance, and yet the concept has remained elusive for many. Personally, I went to the great lengths of becoming my own boss to escape the nine-to-five – only to end up working even more hours, setting up my own business! My experience has led me to the conclusion there is no such thing as work-life balance. There's no separation between work and life: it's all life, and it should all balance. Life doesn't start when work stops; work is a part of life. This is why balance is so important.

Balance concerns our resilience, and how we manage our energy. But what about our perception, and the blurring of the lines between work and life? What can we control in this space, to set better boundaries for ourselves around work and life?

As flexible working becomes more common, we are seeing less commuting and fewer traditional office hours. We can come in to work late if we've got medical appointments or school drop-offs, and leave early if we're logging on that night from home to finish off. We can nip out for yoga over lunchtime when we're working from home, or put a load of washing on and meet a friend for coffee. This is balance, and it happens whilst we work.

At the same time, we're putting more expectation on ourselves to perform – to be noticed despite the reduced face time – and we've blurred the lines between home and work.

Workplace wellness has become big business, and most organisations are well aware of the benefits of employee wellness. Employees who are not well don't deliver optimal performance; it's that simple. As much as wellness initiatives at work can help, though, the free fruit, lunchtime yoga classes and gym memberships will only go so far. Our health is our own responsibility, and we must all be accountable for our wellness – for the benefit of our life, not just our work.

I learned this the hard way. I worked long hours – if I wasn't in meetings, I was in the car. I'd grab fast food because it was quick and I could eat on the run. After getting home late, I was so exhausted exercise was the last thing I felt like doing, so I'd crash on the sofa and then get my laptop out to catch up on emails.

I spent my weekends sleeping in and catching up on all the housework I'd let slide during the week, and I was usually sick during my vacations as my body struggled to cope with the constant demands. I knew my lifestyle wasn't healthy but wasn't sure how to change it; how to find balance. In hindsight, I wasn't in control, and I wasn't prioritising what was important. I never thought about what I needed because I was too busy responding to the needs of others. My goal was always to impress, to be liked, to gain approval. I also thought that working so hard might demonstrate my commitment to peak performance and promotions; again, more was always better – or so I thought. This led to a feeling of overwhelm – that everything was an emergency and needed to be done *now*.

The pressures of our to-do lists feel real, but is everything *really* an emergency? Is everything as urgent on that list as we often treat it? Does everything need to happen today? Do those emails need replying to as soon as they land in your inbox? Does the phone need to be answered each time it rings?

How often does your to-do list reflect things you need to do for *you*? What proportion of it reflects things other people want from you or expect of you? Often the best thing to think about when we're drafting a to-do list is the question 'what do I need?' This might be something quite simple: it doesn't necessarily have to be a day off to go hiking in the hills.

We can all cite examples of important work that turned out not to be so important in the face of real emergencies. The 'important' to-do list items that end up waiting because we have a day off sick. The urgent meeting we miss because the school phones and tells us our child has had an accident. The important business travel that gets cancelled because of an earthquake or pandemic.

Prioritising our workload and managing our priorities is key where burnout and brilliance are concerned.

You may be familiar with the 'big rocks' analogy. I have a jar, some big rocks (representing the most important things I have to do) and some sand (representing all the other things I have to do). How can I fit all this material in the jar (representing the hours in my day)? Most of us will get distracted by the small jobs and put the sand in first; we'll then find we run out of space for the big rocks. If we put the rocks in first, though, we'll find the sand fits between the gaps, allowing ample space in the jar to fit everything in. We can apply this knowledge to the way we schedule our priorities. What are *your* big rocks?

I like to ask myself the following questions: 'Who else can do this?' 'Is it urgent?' 'If I don't do it until tomorrow (or next week), what will happen?'

Rather than prioritising our schedule, we should be scheduling our priorities. By this I mean rather than simply scheduling everything there is to do in priority order selecting the things that matter so the schedule itself is only made of priorities. The real ones, the things that matter.

So how can we apply these lessons?

One of my favourite Buddhist sayings is 'knowing and not doing is the same as not knowing'. In the west we have a thirst for knowledge and learning but the rubber really hits the road when we apply that learning.

I love reading personal development books – but if all I do is read them, nothing changes in my life. For this reason, I like to include practical reflection exercises along the way when I read.

It's a chance for me to consider how I'll apply what I've read and implement the things that resonate, so they make a difference to me, rather than remaining just another thing I intellectually understand.

Here's a chance for you to do the same as we come to the end of this chapter. The following empty table gives you the opportunity to record one thing, for each element of self-care, that you might stop doing, and one thing you might start doing, to help build your resilience and invest in self-care. There may be things you're already doing that you realise now are contributing to your resilience: acknowledge these in the last column.

	STOP	START	KEEP
Mind			
Body (physical)			
Spirit/soul			

BRILLIANT MIND

We've talked about self-care and how we build resilience. This directly impacts our mind-set. In this chapter, we'll look at training the brain: cultivating a clear, calm, positive mind that enables peak performance. This chapter includes some practical tips, to help you manage distractions and rewire your thinking patterns to access a 'flow' state.

First, we have to understand how the mind works and become aware of our own thinking patterns. Cultivating a clear, calm, peak-performing mind is like finely tuning an instrument.

We often refer to highly intelligent people as having a 'brilliant mind'. What does that really mean? What does a mind look like when it's cognitively functioning at its peak? How does that affect what we're able to achieve?

Regardless of intellect, a brilliant mind is one that is rested, clear and calm. It is able to be present and focus; it is therefore sharp and cognitively functioning at its peak.

We've talked about the role of self-care and resilience so far, and the concept of slowing down to speed up. These things also help us cultivate a calmer and more spacious mind. When we can achieve that, we reduce the overwhelm and busyness of our thoughts, and this is key to fine-tuning the way we think, create and perform.

A brilliant mind:

- is sharp and quick

- is aware

- can create and innovate

- is calm and quiet

- knows what it wants

- functions well like a well-tuned instrument

- helps us manage emotions

- is more resilient

- is clear

- is a positive space

- can focus and concentrate with ease

- is a happy place.

The mind is so powerful, and it plays such a critical role in how we show up and how we experience life. The difference between the glass-half-empty people and the glass-half-full people we know is the lens through which they view life. That starts in the mind.

The mind is something we cannot escape from, regardless of how much money we have, how far we travel or how popular we are. Our mind will always be there, and so will the thoughts we put in it, which is why it's important to ensure those thoughts are positive, helpful ones.

We take our thoughts with us everywhere we go. If we're having unhappy thoughts, it doesn't matter if we're at a five-star tropical resort in the sun; we'll still feel unhappy. Or, as monk Matthieu Ricard puts it, 'If you're having suicidal thoughts and someone gives you a luxury penthouse apartment, all you're going to do is look for a window from which to jump.'

Much of the time, we don't even know what's happening in our minds – we're too busy to notice the internal chatter. We're not sure what our minds are up to and whether their activity is helpful for us or not.

Imagine if a megaphone broadcast all our thoughts for the duration of today – what impacts that would have? We'd probably not have a job, many friends or a relationship by the end of the day!

Yet this stuff is going on in there all the time. There can be a barrage of negative self-talk happening in our minds without us even being aware of it.

Our minds are wired to think negatively, so training the mind to think more positively can be an uphill battle: yet it is key to building our resilience.

Many major sports teams have tapped into the power of positive thinking, and many businesses now leverage the power of positive psychology.

After all, positivity begins in the mind. What we think becomes how we feel, and that in turn becomes how we act and the results and outcomes we experience. This is why it's vital our minds are positive – not negative – places.

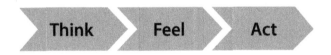

In our busy lives, we are often on autopilot. We get lost in the *doing* at the expense of *being*. Have you ever arrived at work and not remembered the commute? When we are focusing on other things and our minds have wandered, we're not paying attention and life passes us by.

A 2010 *Harvard Business Review* article on multitasking found that the concept is in fact a myth. When our brains are seemingly multitasking, what they're actually doing is switching from one thing to another in very quick succession – often in microseconds.

We must ask ourselves what quality we are giving these simultaneous thoughts when we're multitasking. If we can't actually do many things at once, are we doing our thoughts justice by trying to?

The ideal of multitasking has been ingrained in our culture for a long time – which is why the alternative of slowing down seems so counter-intuitive. Gerry Weinberg explains in his 1992 book *An Introduction to General Systems Thinking*, that frequent switching between tasks costs us on average as much as 40 per cent of our productivity.

In a world where multitasking is seen as a necessary skill, being mindful is the opposite. Mindfulness means slowing down to focus on one thing at a time, one moment at a time, with full concentration and unwavering attention.

Before we can change anything, we need to understand how the mind works, and become aware of what's going on in there.

THE NEUROSCIENCE OF MINDSET

Our brains are so busy. One of the reasons we feel so overwhelmed is the amount of information rushing through our mind at any given time. Research tells us that we generally have between 60,000 and 90,000 thoughts during the course of a day: it's a lot to process. Among those thousands of thoughts are all the things we have to do, all the worries we have, our assumptions as to what others think of us, our regrets of the past and our plans for the future.

When we think about how busy our lives have become, how much there is on our schedule and the expectations we place on ourselves, both at home and at work, it can be overwhelming.

Sometimes the mind feels full of fog: there are a million and one things buzzing around in there, and we don't have the space to think about any of them clearly.

The mind has always amazed me. Through following a decade of studies in mindfulness across the world, I've come to understand the power of our minds, how we treat them and the impact our minds have on everything we do.

Our state of mind affects our perspective, how we face challenges, how we treat ourselves and others, the beliefs we hold, the confidence we have in ourselves, how we show up and, of course, how well we perform.

The brain has 86 billion neurons, all capable of firing different neural pathways. The ones that fire together generally wire together, but so often we're not conscious of just what those are. We're unaware of the quality of the well-worn pathways in our brains we're forming day after day, and the thinking patterns that are driving us: our thoughts about how good we are, what others think of us, what we should or shouldn't do, how we look, and whether we're good enough.

The good news is that the plasticity of the brain means we can literally rewire those neural pathways and form new thought patterns – making the mind a better place to be.

Our brains are predisposed to think negatively. It's how we've evolved, and we use negative thinking to keep us safe. If we're constantly scanning the horizon for the worst that can happen, we are able to prepare for it and react to it. This helped us survive back in the days of saber-toothed tigers. In our modern life though, our negative thinking patterns can be harmful: we tend to notice all the things we don't like about ourselves, the things we want but that we've not got yet, and what's not gone well for us at work.

This tendency to focus on the negative is like watering a garden full of weeds: you just get bigger weeds. So the saying goes, what you focus on grows.

If I ask you to think of one negative thing that's happened this week, it'll probably come to you quite easily: something that didn't go well; someone who upset you? Chances are you'll have been thinking about it for days since it happened and ruminating on it at night. Now, if I ask you the same question about something positive, you'll probably find it harder to recall. Even if the positives outweigh the negatives for you in a particular week, it's the negatives you remember and reflect on.

Dr Barbara Fredrickson's study on positivity ratios found that, to offset the negativity bias that exists in the brain, we need a ratio of 3:1. That's three positive thoughts, emotions or experiences to every one negative.

There's a lot of work to be done in this space. Our negativity bias is like a well-worn walking track: we use it regularly, so it's smooth and easy to navigate. To even this out, we need to start firing more of the positive neural pathways and breaking down a less-travelled path in the brain, an overgrown track. You know those huts you find up in the mountains after days of hiking? Positive thoughts can feel like these tracks; the chances are the climb is more difficult to navigate, overgrown and steep.

How can we counter the negativity bias and train our brains to become a more positive place to be? It takes time, like training a muscle. We don't go into the gym for the first time and pick up the heaviest weight. A similar principle applies to training our brains. It's not an overnight thing; we start small and build up. It takes practice.

This retraining is about rewiring the neural pathways in our brain to see things more evenly. The more we fire those positive neural pathways, the more we'll even out the bias. A more even, positive distribution of thoughts will become our default state. When we can achieve this, it's not our life that will change, but the lens through which we view it. We'll start to see the positives as well as the negatives.

I'm in the habit of thinking of three things I'm grateful for every morning. Another of the tools I use to fire those positive neural pathways in my brain is a success diary. This is my favourite strategy, and I started it because I had a poor memory and wanted to prepare better for my annual performance reviews. I began to write down the successes I experienced throughout my working year. I found that I got a lift each time I reflected on them. It provided evidence to offset my negativity bias and a place I could go on my 'off' days when my mindset was more 'half empty' than 'half full'. These days, it's an icon on my desktop, because I've advanced technologically over the years. Choose what works for you: an inbox folder, a desktop icon, an old-fashioned paper journal or even a corkboard in your office.

Every time we add to a success diary, we're walking down those overgrown tracks and helping our brain retrain to see more of the positive. The negative will still be there, but its voice won't be as loud, because we've trained ourselves to see a more even distribution of reality that includes some positives too.

The external world doesn't change but the way we view it does and we start to see a more accurate reflection of reality not one that's heavily weighted towards our negativity bias.

What we focus on grows – so what kind of mindset are *your* thinking patterns cultivating?

Regardless of your answer to this question, there's likely to be days when your mind is not your friend: this is part of being human. Part of my job is public speaking – and sometimes, I share the stage with other speakers I admire and respect. I know that one day I can be inspired by these successful people, and the next day I can feel threatened by them. The feeling is all down to my mindset.

Self talk and the inner critic is a struggle sometimes – and often locked away in our subconscious. So what can we do about it?

UNDERSTANDING THINKING PATTERNS

One of the things I quickly understood through learning to meditate was the power of watching my thoughts: not just noticing them, but learning what was going on inside my head and stilling the tide to the point where I could create space. Space to think more thoughts, as it turns out!

You are not your thoughts, but your thoughts have a massive impact on how you feel and your resulting experiences. That's why it's so important to be in control of our thoughts – but also great news; our thoughts don't have to define us.

If I was to tell you three years before COVID that there would ever be a queue outside a New Zealand supermarket to get inside it, you'd think I was crazy. We certainly wouldn't have imagined ourselves going and standing in that queue: it just wasn't something we would have ever expected to do. Now that sort of thing has become the norm, and something we all do without questioning. A similar effect is at play in terms of our busyness, the hours we work as a marker of our productivity and the scarcity approach to marketing that makes us feel 'less than' and convinces us we need to buy more to fix ourselves. It's easy to see how our thoughts can be manipulated, and to feel like we have no control over them.

I liken our thinking patterns to the cultivation of a garden. What we water grows – that can be either beautiful flowers or unwanted weeds. If we water the weeds and negative thoughts, we end up with a mind full of out-of-control weeds, with no room for the beautiful flowers to bloom.

This can certainly be true in the case of stress. We often think of stress as having external causes. It's people or situations that stress us out. Yet, in reality, stress is our response to something external. For example, a traffic jam is only stressful if you're running late; someone else can be in the same jam and not feel stressed by it. It's not the jam that's the problem, it's our reaction to it. The same applies to our interactions with our kids; they can act up one day and we'll let it slide, but if they do the same thing after a hard day at work following an argument with our spouse, we'll likely lose it. It's not the acting up that's stressful, it's our response – based on how resilient we feel, how tired we are and what else is going on in our life. If it rains and I'm in the city without a rain coat, I find it stressful, but if I'm at home and the water tank is low it's anything but – same rain, different response. Stress is caused by our internal responses.

The good news about this is that it means we have the power to do something about stress. We can't control the external circumstances, but we can control our response: the point at which a factor becomes either stressful or not.

Handling or avoiding stress is all about our thinking patterns – and many of these patterns have been formed over years, without us being consciously aware of them. We have two influencing factors where thoughts are concerned, those that come from internally (the most common and powerful) and those that come externally (which can influence our internal patterns if we're exposed to them long enough).

As an example: I always struggled with imposter syndrome (or imposter experience, as I prefer to call it, because it's a state of mind and a passing experience rather than a medical syndrome). In my corporate career it was because I didn't have a degree. My internal thought pattern was that I wasn't as clever as everyone else. However, this was matched by the external commentary around the leadership table that we should only hire degree qualified leaders. Despite performing well and matching those around the table in terms of contribution these beliefs were contributing to my feelings of imposterism and that only degree qualified people were clever enough to be leaders.

Despite the external messages that influence our thoughts

(especially when we're young), nothing is more powerful than the messages we give ourselves. The stories we tell ourselves and the things we believe can either prevent change from happening or allow new skills to develop. As Henry Ford said, 'whether you think you can or you think you can't, you're probably right'.

This was brought home to me recently during an experience that terrified me unnecessarily: a great example of our thinking patterns at work. I was heading to see a client in the Wellington CBD, and found a parking spot along the busy Terrace. The problem was that I needed to reverse into the space: something that always fills me with dread, especially on a busy road. Still, it was the only spot, so I accordingly began my parking manoeuvre.

The already tense situation became much worse when, as I was concentrating on the park, a man suddenly opened the passenger door , picked up my bag on the seat and attempted to get in the car.

I froze, I panicked and I think I said something along the lines of 'what the f**k are you doing in my car?!' Was I going to have a knife held to my throat? Was I being robbed? Or worse? All kinds of things went through my head in moments.

The man turned to look at me and said 'Sorry, wrong car! I thought you were my lift.' He'd been waiting by the open parking space for his partner.

He quickly jumped out and I completed my park, still shaking.

Why do I share this? To show the way our brains form our beliefs and how this affects our reactions and our assumptions. Neurons that fire together wire together: our previous experiences also help form these neural pathways; we use them for reference when similar events play out.

I'm aware I can't reverse park very well. It was the reason I failed my first driving test, and something I've told myself ever since that I can't do. I always get worried when I reverse park – it's a well-worn track in my brain that I reinforce every time I do it. I think, 'oh great, I need to reverse park, and it's a busy road, in front of all these people. I'm probably going to stuff it up.'

I've also watched way too many movies of women being attacked by men – although, to be fair, there are a lot of similar, real stories in the news too! My neural pathways have formed to reflect strange men approaching my car as a threat: a likely robbery or some kind of violence or harm. Even though this has never been the case for me, it has been for thousands of other women, so it, too, is a well-worn track in my brain. We form the pathways in our brain based on what we consume, as well as our real-life experiences (consider your social media and Netflix diet here).

Neurons firing together, equating risk and fear, was the reason my go-to response in this situation was to think the worst. My fight-or-flight response further reduced my capacity to analyse what was going on and think of other logical explanations. In that split second, the answer is always going to be 'imminent danger' over 'maybe an innocent mistake'.

So what neurons tend to fire together in *your* brain, and where are the well-worn tracks? What are they telling you? It might be 'I can't do this' or 'They're going to find me out.' It might be 'She's better at this than I am' or 'I don't know if this is good enough.'

We can rewire our brains; form new neural pathways and encourage a better story, more confidence, less fear. We can encourage neurons to fire together in a way that help us recognise our abilities, celebrate our successes and think more positively.

REFRAMING

The first step in retraining our brains is to become aware, to pay attention and to begin to understand the thinking patterns we've formed. Once we know that, we can decide which patterns are helpful and which ones we need to change. We can do this by reframing or calling out unhelpful thoughts as they arise.

Cognitive reframing is a technique you can use to shift your mindset so you're able to look at a situation from a slightly different perspective. It's a psychological technique that consists of identifying and then changing the way we view situations, experiences and ideas.

The aim of reframing is to shift our perspective to empower us to act.

A common, well-known frame is the half-full glass – and, conversely, the half-empty glass. It's the same glass we're looking at, but the views are different.

When we notice negative thoughts or feelings, we have an opportunity to employ reframing. Strategies to help us do this include the '*Yes, but' technique*, where the goal is to counter negative thoughts with positive ones. For example, we might say, '*Yes*, I just lost my job, *but* I have a lot of experience and skills that employers are looking for.'

We can also simply ask 'what are the facts here?' or 'How might someone else look at this?' 'What is the evidence?' In the face of 'I'm not achieving enough in my first week of my new job; they'll think they've made the wrong hire', the answers to these questions become: 'I'm learning; no one expects me to know it all in week one. I'm fully capable of proving my credibility in good time.'

Reframing does not mean denying that there's a challenge or saying that we shouldn't be struggling. It's not an attempt to convince ourselves that everything should always be rosy. It's a tool to shift our perspective and obtain a more helpful, positive view on a given situation. Reframing can help us change our point of view, gain perspective, validate our emotions and, most importantly, separate emotions from facts.

When we are aware of our thoughts we can identify areas for improvement: we can take a thought, reframe it and make it positive. Here are some examples:

- I've no idea what I'm doing – I'm going to learn a lot.

- I don't know if I can do this – I'm fully capable of growing into this job.

- I'm scared about the unknown – I'm excited about the opportunities.

- She always has the best ideas – Ideas are her strengths; I have other strengths.

Sometimes the most helpful thing we can do if we're unable to reframe a thought is to become aware of it and then, each time it comes up, make an effort to let it go; to call it out as an unhelpful thought and to practise allowing it to pass rather than letting it hold sway with us.

Spending a few minutes a day watching your thoughts is an interesting exercise. We might feel it is unproductive, but it can hold great insights for us. How can we change our thinking patterns if we've no idea what they are? This is the first step.

Perhaps your thought patterns take the form of a jealous voice that compares you to others. Maybe it's the 'I'm not good enough' thought that keeps cropping up for you, or the 'what if I fail' pattern, or 'I'm not worthy'. We have so many thoughts, and we're all different – but by watching what goes on in our mind we quickly start to realise which ones are holding us back.

For example, there might have been a promotion you let pass you by recently: you left it too late or didn't call the managers back to book an interview. You're not really sure why – perhaps it was the thought 'I'm not sure I can do this' repeating over and over in your subconscious. Or you might have neglected to challenge a colleague, because of the thinking pattern 'they know more than me' or 'it's not my place to disagree'.

When we become aware of our mind and cultivate the ability to train it, we find we open up space: space to think in, create in, have ideas in and solve problems in. This, of course, directly affects our performance.

PRACTICAL STRATEGIES TO CULTIVATE MINDSET

We've explored the neuroscience of our negativity bias and our thinking patterns. We've learned how to reframe our thoughts. What else makes a brilliant mind? How can we cultivate a mindset that enables us to reach our potential?

In my experience, the two biggest differences I've made cognitively have been through stilling my mind and being more present and aware. Both of these skills I've cultivated through regular meditation.

A mind that is still and aware can think more clearly, innovate and respond rather than react. It is also a calmer, more pleasant place to be. It's easier for me to be a glass-half-full kind of person with an organised, clear, calm mind producing my thoughts. It's also easier for me to perform well if I can solve problems, make decisions and have a clear head. This also helps with focus and concentration, which we'll talk more about towards the end of this chapter. But first, how do we master our mindset and cultivate calmness and clarity?

Mindfulness by definition is awareness; it's being in the present and focusing on one thing at a time, one moment at a time.

When we rest our minds and still them by being present and mindful, our minds become a more positive place. We're then able to hear the important stuff through the noise of the busyness. Mindfulness doesn't have to come through meditating either; being present is enough. Watching the sunset, becoming aware of our breathing, writing in a gratitude journal or catching a wave surfing are all examples of being mindfully aware and in the present.

Before we can cultivate a positive mindset, we must make room in our mind and calm its busyness. If our minds are busy and full, we struggle to think straight.

Learning how to control our mind is an essential part of peak performance. This is not just about learning to calm the busy thoughts and become more clear – it's about focus, creativity and mental sharpness. It's like the warrant of fitness on a car to ensure it doesn't break down and drives well – or tuning a guitar to ensure it produces a beautiful sound when we play it.

So how can we start to cultivate a mindset for peak performance? How do we tune our brain so it can perform at its peak?

For me, cultivating a mindset for peak performance is about having a toolkit to tap into when my brain becomes busy. Deep breaths are in my toolkit (I take a few each morning before I begin my day); so is a few moments to recentre (which I do after a tough meeting). When we still our minds, the important stuff floats to the top, rather than the noise of all the busyness we're constantly faced with.

When we do this, we also begin to notice what our inner voice is saying. Have you ever stopped to think about the way you talk to yourself? It's probably a way you'd never dream of talking to another human being. Be your own best friend, and keep an eye on that inner critic.

The first few years of my meditation practice involved a constant practising of focus: a back and forth of thinking and not thinking. I kept getting distracted and then coming back. This is actually the art of meditation, it's how we hone our concentration. We train the brain to return to the present each time a stray thought takes it away. The nature of our minds is to think – so thoughts will always be there.

Sitting in a garden overlooking a field of sunflowers in the south of France, I finally learned the power of the space between our thoughts, and what happens when we access this space.

I've been on a number of silent retreats where, apart from eat and sleep, all we do is meditate. Such retreats deliver an opportunity for constant practice of thinking in the stillness and training our brains to focus, to be present, to be aware. It's basically hours of taming the wandering mind. From my experience of these retreats, here are my top tips for practising the art of concentration.

- Spend time in stillness and quiet regularly.
- Become aware.
- Observe your thoughts (without analysing or attaching to them).
- Notice distractions and practise concentration by bringing your focus back to the present.

The best practical strategies to train the brain are all really the same thing: whether we call it mindfulness, meditation or conscious breathing, it's the art of being in the present: practising concentration on one thing at a time and finding stillness. It sounds so easy, yet it can be very difficult to achieve in a world that prioritises busyness, doing and noise. Simply sitting still and noticing your breath, or noticing five things that are going on around you, is practising being present. As with any other skill, the more we practise, the better we get. Each time we focus on the present and still the mind we're cultivating a brilliant mind.

MANAGING DISTRACTIONS

It makes sense for us to look after our minds and make an effort to rest them, but how often do we spend time taking care of them?

In fact, we tend to do the opposite – we spend time filling our minds with social media feeds, bad news stories, rubbish TV, stress, worries about the future and regrets about the past.

Everything we put into our minds has an impact on the kind of mindset we're cultivating. This includes the people we hang out with, the gossip we engage in, the news we watch, the TV shows we consume and, of course, our social media diet.

Our relationship with technology impacts our mindset massively, so we can't not talk about it here.

Technology has revolutionised the way we live and work, but we are now starting to see the mental health impacts of our constant connection to devices and the way it overloads our already busy brains.

Now, I don't think technology is bad. It's amazing, and it has some real life-improving uses: keeping in touch with friends and family overseas, disaster management, health apps and more spring to mind. Technology is important for my business – but it's also important that, for my health and performance, I'm careful about the amount of time I spend using it.

It's not so much technology that's the problem, but rather our relationship with it. Like everything, in moderation it can be good, but that's the problem – we've never been very good at moderation as humans in the developed world.

In tough times like the COVID-19 pandemic, technology is our way of keeping informed. However, we can have a tendency to overload our brains with information, or to keep refreshing our feeds in the hope of better news.

If we can use our devices, rather than having them use us, we'll be a lot healthier and happier.

We know that spending too much time on our devices is not good for stress and our focus, and that it makes us feel more exhausted. Quite simply put, overuse of technology compromises our brain and detracts from peak performance.

Before the advent of smartphones, we used to have many pauses during our normal day: these gave us a little time to rest and reset the mind. Waiting for the kettle to boil, waiting for the bus to arrive, waiting for the lift to the next floor, waiting in the supermarket queue. Now, during those times in which our minds used to be idling, resting and checking in with ourselves, we're absorbing many more thoughts, emotions and information instead.

Most people report their minds feeling busy, full and overloaded; some even go as far as to describe themselves as crazy, stressed, anxious or depressed. Scrolling through social media for four hours a day is going to make this worse, not better.

Our phones are often the first thing we reach for when we wake up. We might have looked at the weather forecast, checked the news headlines, replied to friends' messages, watched a few cat videos, scrolled through some Instagram photos and liked a few Facebook posts all before we've even got out of bed. If that's the case, just think about how much information we've just placed in our busy brain before we've even thought about the day ahead and the things we have to do – and we wonder why we can't think straight!

A similar routine might play out at the end of the day, when we go to bed – and we wonder why we struggle to sleep.

According to recent findings, an average person checks their phone about 63 times a day.

Eighty-seven per cent of us do it one hour before going to bed, and 69 per cent of us do it within the first five minutes of waking up.

When we're lost in our device, we're less present and, as a result, much more distracted – to the point where some of us can't cross the road safely any more, such is our attachment to our device and our connection to the virtual world.

We live in a digitally distracted world. Technology is key to the way we live our life, yet it affects our mental health and our ability to perform.

So how do we balance this?

I've removed my notifications – I check my emails or Facebook once or twice a day, with a sense of more conscious intention. I've not been tricked into logging on for the tenth time that day because of a red notification badge. This also means that, if I pick my phone up to check the weather, I don't get distracted by a notification and find myself 30 minutes later watching videos of baby goats.

Allow your device to monitor your usage, and set goals or downtime periods so your device is actually helping you develop healthier habits. Use the data the device collects to be aware of how much you're using your device and specific apps on it, and use this knowledge to formulate an idea of what's reasonable for you.

Set times for checking messages and media – maybe once in the morning and then once after lunch – and resolve not to pick up your device between times. Don't keep it close to hand. Have device-free zones in the house. The dinner table and the bedroom are great starting points. Alternatively, a 'no-devices-after-9-pm' rule might work for your family.

Don't take your device to bed. I know this is hard when so many of us use it as an alarm, but it's worth finding a way around that. If it's in the bedroom, it's likely to be the first thing we look at and the last thing we do before sleep. Devices' LED screens interrupt our melatonin production, and therefore interfere with our sleep. If we wake up in the middle of the night, the worst thing we can do is start scrolling, if we want to get back to sleep.

Going to bed is supposed to be the time when we slow down the brain, begin to unplug and switch off. If we're scrolling through the news, checking our emails, putting filters on our selfies and comparing our life to what other people are posting, imagine what that fills our brain with just before we're supposed to be seeking sleep.

This is even more important where our work device is concerned, because the information input becomes much more stressful and overwhelming if it's work emails and staff conversations on Slack invading our bedroom at night.

Yes, we all have busy lives and face challenges in the real world, but that's even more reason to create space in our brain: when we can do this, we can process and deal with the challenges, rather than busying our minds further through our device habits and information overload.

I declare a device-free day once a month. On this day, I switch off my phone and put it in a drawer, even if it's just from 8 am to 8 pm on a Sunday. It's amazing what a break my mind gets when I do this – and how much more time I find in the day to do other things.

Peak performance requires a clear, calm, focused mind – and too much scrolling on our devices compromises this.

If we clear our minds of busy thoughts and cultivate clarity, we find we're closer to the state of flow, which I'm about to explore. It's another key component of peak performance and our ability to focus.

FOCUS AND FLOW

Have you ever found yourself so completely immersed in a task that hours flew by you unnoticed? Or been so absorbed in what you were doing that the doing itself became the goal? This state is often when we're feeling most energised and accomplished; it's the effortless state of performance known as flow.

'Flow' is an optimal state of presence and consciousness, in which we feel our best and perform at our best. As part of my discussion about achieving brilliance, I'm going to explore this concept of flow and guide you to achieving it more regularly.

We've talked about mindset, and how to cultivate a brilliant mind. The techniques I talked about in that regard are great training for accessing a state of flow, which relies on a mind that is clear, present and focused. In other words, a brilliant mind enables flow.

Fortune 500 companies, US Navy SEALs and elite sports teams all teach their people how to trigger flow, to ensure cutting-edge performances.

When we're in flow, it's likely we'll feel full of energy; our productivity will increase; we'll be more creative and innovative; and we'll feel more confident and happier.

Flow researcher and author Steven Kotler reports that flow can increase creativity by 400 per cent and learning uptake by 240–500 per cent.

In a 10-year McKinsey study, top executives reported being five times more productive in flow. That would mean that if we spent Monday in flow we could literally take the rest of the week off and still have got more done than most people.

The same study estimated that most of us spend less than 5 per cent of our work life in flow. If that number could be nudged up closer to 20 per cent, according to the study, overall workplace productivity would almost double. That's a significant shift on the dial where performance is concerned.

Research by flow guru Mihaly Csikszentmihalyi concludes there are eight characteristics of flow:
1. complete concentration on the task
2. clarity of goals and reward in mind and immediate feedback
3. transformation of time

4. the experience being intrinsically rewarding
5. effortlessness
6. a balance between challenge and skills
7. actions and awareness being merged; loss of self-conscious rumination
8. a feeling of control over the task.

Csikszentmihalyi tells us that, to create flow, an activity must stretch our potential enough for there to be an even balance between how challenging the activity feels for us and our level of skill to complete the activity. This is known as the challenge to skill ratio and Csikszentmihalyi's model is pictured below.

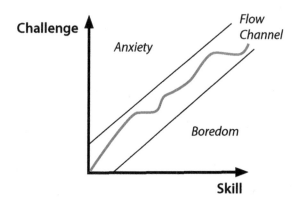

People in flow describe it as being 'in the zone', 'totally absorbed' in the task, oblivious to everything going on around them and being at one with the activity. Flow is often attributed to athletes and artists – but it's available to us all.

We can find flow in those moments of focus when we're using our skills, being stretched enough to feel challenged and accomplished, creating something with meaning and feeling totally absorbed in that. Flow is about achievable challenge; we won't be in flow when things are too easy or boring; nor will we be in flow when we're out of our depth or worried we can't do the task at hand. When we are in flow we're in control and we know we're capable too.

People who experience flow describe it as 'timeless'. They say they feel content, serene, focused and completely involved, and forget all else. They experience a connection to something bigger through what they're doing, and inner clarity.

Flow for me is when my mind is clear. It's in the moment and it's fully focused on one thing, the task at hand. The chaos of busyness that exists when my mind is multitasking and full of thoughts has subsided.

I particularly notice the difference between being in flow and not being in that state when I write. A blog post I'm battling with can sometimes take days to get right – and then other times I'll have an idea whilst out walking the dog, and I'll come back and sit at my laptop and absorb myself in the task of getting it down. I'll write the best post ever in about 20 minutes. I'm totally absorbed in it; the thoughts literally flow from my pen (or laptop keys), and I know it's good. I can forget lunchtime when this happens (which for such a foodie is highly unusual) and it's when I'm at my happiest at work.

Having a goal is important, but flow is about enjoying the journey and not just fixating on the end product. When you're in flow it's important to allow yourself to simply live in the present moment without worrying too much about the ultimate outcome of your efforts.

We only have a finite amount of attention and focus: if we're spreading them across many activities, it makes sense we're not going to achieve the same level of quality. If we're attending a meeting whilst thinking about what's for dinner, reading the notes from the last meeting and checking our emails, all of those activities are going to be compromised. If we focus all of our energy or attention on one thing, the quality will improve dramatically.

Flow is like mindfulness, which I've long thought is the secret to success is so many ways.

When we succumb to the flurry of thoughts running through our head, our minds become chaotic, and we get more and more distracted.

A 2016 study conducted at the US National Institute on Aging found that allowing our mind to be disorganised doesn't just feel bad – it's also actually bad for us. A disorganised mind leads to high stress and chronic negativity.

This reminds me of my yoga teacher training. When doing balancing poses we're always told to find a gaze point ('Drishti' in Sanskrit, meaning 'focused gaze', used to develop concentrated intention). When we focus our eyes on one, non-moving thing, we find balance so much easier, and our concentration improves. When we're looking around the room at everyone else, we wobble much more. When we focus on one thing at a time, we make a better job of it.

TIPS TO CREATE FLOW

- Practise mindfulness – a present mind is a focused one.
- Do things that use your skills/strengths.
- Develop healthy habits (in terms of sleeping, eating and moving).
- Look for a healthy level of challenge and stretch.
- Take regular breaks.
- Avoid distractions.

The reason we want to be in flow is because when we're in that state we are at our best, we are most focused, we're undisturbed and we're therefore giving 100 per cent to what we're doing.

Flow also allows us to access 'deep work': a phrase coined by Cal Newport, a *professor* at Georgetown University and a New York Times best-selling author.

In his book *Deep Work*, Newport describes the concept as 'professional activities performed in a state of distraction free concentration that push your cognitive capabilities to their limit. These efforts create new value, improve your skill and are hard to replicate.'

Like flow, deep work is the ability to focus without distraction on a cognitively demanding task. It's a skill that allows us to quickly master complicated information and produce better results in less time.

Deep work is about carving out the thinking space to come up with our best ideas. Perhaps on one of those trips to the golf course we all thought were a waste of company time!

If we're constantly stuck in the *doing*, we don't give our brains space to do the *thinking* – which is where our innovation comes from. Yes, we need implementation – but if we don't leave space for thinking there's nothing great to implement.

I'll often take myself off to the beach for the day, or go kayaking or for a bush walk. To most people it probably looks like a day off. I'm pretty sure my wife doesn't think I'm working on those days! However, this is a key part of my job and it's central to my success. This is my thinking space. It's where I create, have ideas or mull over problems. What might look in the diary like a day off can result in my biggest breakthroughs or my next best seller. My brain can't achieve what it does at these times if I'm in the office checking emails. It requires the space to tap into its most innovative capacity, and it's from that capacity that these valuable thoughts flow.

It can feel counterintuitive to diary thinking time; space to sit and ponder. In a society that has prioritised busy and doing, to take time to think and do nothing (especially on company time) can feel indulgent. Yet it's critical to our success, and it's also an element of performing at our peak to have this space. Putting time in your diary for thinking space makes you better at your job. In fact, if you're a leader it is part of your job.

According to Newport, deep work makes us better at what we do, but our environments and equipment are not always enablers of this type of work. Most of us have lost the art of going deep – or we don't allow ourselves the space.

We have to be intentional about getting into this state, otherwise we run the risk of busying our way through our to-do list and only ever being in a 'shallow work' mode.

This is one of the reasons I schedule retreats for myself. I go away to plan my year ahead. I go away to write. It's usually just me in a rural Airbnb somewhere with no distractions. I put my phone away, turn my notifications off and don't check emails. This allows me the space to think, to create and to do deep work.

It's also why I was never a fan of the open plan office (that and being an introvert). I always struggled to go into a state of deep work and fully focus with so many distractions around me.

It turned out that managed isolation and quarantine was a great distraction-free environment for deep work. In fact, that is where I wrote this book: it was a way I could use my time productively whilst in quarantine. There were no distractions; I couldn't do anything other than write. (Having said that, though, the situation was missing some of the usual environmental factors I need for creativity – like fresh air and sunshine).

We don't have to go on retreat, hit the golf course or even leave the office to do deep work. All we need is an environment within which we can focus. When I'm doing deep work, my phone is always on silent; I let my voicemail pick up calls and return them later.

But don't just take my advice. Newport himself advises we focus on four elements to achieve deep work:

1. location

2. duration

3. structure

4. requirements.

Focusing on location might mean you decide to work at home, with the office door closed. Setting a duration means you can intentionally allow for a focus on deep work for a certain amount of time. 'Structure' refers to the set-up that makes it happen (for example, putting the phone away and the computer on do not disturb until you've written 10,000 words). 'Requirements' refers to the final touches, the things you need to make the deep work a success. It might be having water nearby and the laptop charger plugged in, or putting your favourite music on your headphones to help you focus.

It makes sense that the more time we can spend in flow or deep working, the more likely it is we'll be effective and performing at our peak.

Of course, this can be easier said than done – a lot of the success of these strategies will come down to the actions we take and the habits we form.

Let's look next at the key indicators for peak performance, and how we can learn to cultivate the habits that lead to that state.

FOUNDATIONS OF PEAK PERFORMANCE

We're on the home straight. So far, we've explored what got us here in the first place and how to develop a new relationship with busy. We've looked at building our resilience and keeping burnout at bay. We've explored what's realistic and the imperfection that exists within brilliance.

So how does brilliance relate to peak performance, and how do we get there? Is peak performance even a destination, or is it perhaps more about the journey?

Now we've developed the mindset for brilliance, let's work to understand the foundations for peak performance. What characterises a high performer, and how does peak performance contribute to their brilliance?

In this chapter we'll explore the importance of strengths, the role of habits and the way tiny gains can contribute to brilliant results.

For each individual, brilliance looks different, because by virtue of being human we're all different in terms of our skill sets, personality traits and thinking preferences. But when it comes to studying peak performance, there are some common themes.

Take something like leadership: leadership entails many different skills, and most leaders probably won't have all of them – but they'll certainly excel in a certain area if they're a high-performing leader. If we put a handful of successful leaders into a room it's unlikely they'd have the same skillset. Some would be stronger in empathy, communication, delivering results or strategic vision but they'd all be high performing.

Whatever our skills are, they help us perform in a way that fits our unique ability, experience and character.

Peak performance entails the abilities to set goals and consider the future, respond to and manage change, build resilience, reflect so we can continue to learn and grow, collaborate and be open to views and ideas of others. Self-awareness is vital too, as is the careful balance between challenging ourselves and having the support to succeed (this includes being able to ask for help too).

Assuming we've got the required skills and capability in the first place, achieving our potential requires a combination of our awareness of and belief in those skills (self-efficacy) and the energy to perform (resilience). This is the recipe for brilliance and how we achieve our potential.

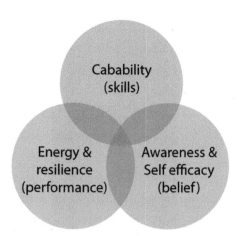

We've talked about energy and resilience, and we'll go on to talk about self-belief and confidence, but right now I want us to talk about strengths and skills: probably the most obvious elements of performance.

KNOW YOUR STRENGTHS

Global analytics experts Gallup has surveyed 26 million people using their StrengthsFinder assessment, which is backed by 50 years of research. (You can take this assessment yourself online.) Results have shown that if we focus on our strengths, we'll be six times more likely to be engaged at work, 8 per cent more productive and three times more likely to have an excellent quality of life. It's no wonder, given this data, Gallup advocates for a strengths-based approach.

Strengths are important, yet we often ignore them in favour of focusing on what we need to work on or improve. As a nation, New Zealanders can err on the side of modesty. We can find it difficult or embarrassing to accept compliments; we are conditioned to be modest and not to promote our abilities.

Strengths can be a tricky area, because strengths feel effortless. If we're good at something, we tend to find it easy, so we assume our particular strength is nothing special: everyone must find it easy. We underrate the impact of our strength and don't think it's worthy of a mention. This, combined with the negativity bias I've discussed and concerns about modesty, is a perfect storm for undervaluing our strengths.

Yet knowing what our strengths are and leveraging them are crucial aspects of peak performance. To use a sporting analogy, we all had our favourite position in the school sports team, likely because we were good at it – shooting, defending or goalkeeping. When a player plays out of their favoured position, their performance isn't as good: performance is about playing to our strengths.

Unfortunately, where our work is concerned, we are predisposed to focus on the things we're *not* good at, rather than the things we are. As I've discussed, our brains are predisposed to think negatively.

We're also very quick in the modern world to move on to the next thing – we don't spend time reflecting on the positive, what went well, why and what strengths we used to achieve our successes.

Research has proven that focusing on our strengths helps us perform at our peak, but first we have to know what our strengths are.

Stop for a minute and write down a list of your strengths – all the things you're good at. What feedback have you received at work? What did they tell you they'd miss about you when you left your last company? What would those who know you well describe as your top five strengths?

EXERCISE

My top five strengths are:

1. ....

2. ....

3. ....

4. ....

Others tell me my strengths are:

1. ....

2. ....

3. ....

4. ....

5. ....

Some of the ways these strengths play out are:

Focusing on our strengths takes less energy than focusing on our weaknesses, and is far more enjoyable. We're never going to be good at everything, and nine times out of ten there are other people in the team who are good at the things we're not, and vice versa. The power of a team is in recognising complementary skill sets and leveraging different strengths.

Roger Federer played both tennis and basketball growing up. Obviously, he was very good at tennis. He chose to focus on that, and leverage his strength in this sport. Eventually he turned tennis into his career, rather than focusing his time and energy on trying to get better at basketball.

Yes, we may need to give some attention to our weaknesses sometimes, but overall, we achieve our potential by leveraging our strengths.

Gallup tells me that one of my top five strengths is discipline. That resonates with me: it's how I remain consistent in my business and also how I've managed to write five books all within their deadline. It's something I didn't ever realise was a strength until Gallup made me aware of it: I just thought everyone had as much discipline as I did.

My discipline helps me form good habits and stick to a routine. The habits we have are so often a predetermining factor in our success on the quest for peak performance.

THE ROLE OF HABITS

'We are what we repeatedly do. Excellence therefore is not an
act but a habit' – Aristotle

Often the difference between those who succeed and those who do
not is the habits they form. This is how we hit peak performance –
forming good habits and breaking bad ones.

All Blacks mental skills coach, Gilbert Enoka, talks about this
in relating his experience of coaching rugby players. There's a
combination of mindset and skillset he says is crucial for success,
but there's also a third, equally important point: structure. Together,
mindset, skillset and structure make up Enoka's success triangle.

He's witnessed players who have the necessary skills and mindset
still fail to make the team because of a lack of structure. If they
can't adhere to the necessary routine of training, early nights, meal
plans and habits, they will inevitably not succeed.

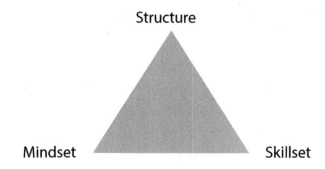

Of course, the fact that habits are so important is easier said
than done. Often it's not our lack of knowledge that's the problem
but how we implement the knowledge we do have, especially on a
regular basis. Success requires structure, in the form of a succession
of positive habits.

Forming good habits sounds simple, but, of course, it's not. Otherwise, we'd all go to the gym, eat salad all the time and wake up at 6 am every day. Even when we know the negative impacts of a certain habit, it can be hard to break. Think of smoking, for example; we all know it kills us, but sometimes that's still not enough to stop us.

A habit is a repeated behaviour that becomes automatic. The trouble is that we tend to find it easier to keep the bad habits and harder to form good ones – that involves more effort and less immediate reward.

Our bad habits work against us by being easy to perform and giving us instant reward hits – a wine on a Friday night, for example. Eating well, in contrast, won't give us an immediate sugar hit, and the health benefits or weight loss might not be evident until weeks down the track.

How can we build positive habits and break bad ones? The best advice I've heard on this topic comes from James Clear in his book *Atomic Habits*. Clear believes that both success and failure are preceded by habits, and that we can be the *creator*, rather than the victim, of our habits. What's on our desk or the way we set up our home can influence our behaviours and habits, he says; our environment is the architect of our habits.

What I like about focusing on our habits is that it puts us in control; it's something we can influence. Whilst we tend to think that success is just down to talent, and that some people are just high performers for that reason, there's much more to it. Talent gets us so far, but great habits make the difference. It makes sense when we look at those who are truly talented. At some point, those people are going to reach a peak at which everyone else around them is just as talented. At that point, how do they stand out? The answer lies in good habits, continuous improvement and a drive for performance. A lot of top athletes, for example, may have had talent to start with

– but so did others who've not made it in their field. The difference most of these athletes talk about is the hard work and effort they've put in.

Peak performance is about forming good habits and repeating them consistently, whether that's a gym routine, organising your diary, doing your filing, taking a lunch break or checking in on the team.

Let's look at breaking bad habits first.

Reducing exposure and temptation is fundamental. If you want to save money, unsubscribe from those marketing emails that tempt you with specials. Want to stop eating chocolate at night whilst watching TV? Don't buy it or have it in the house. If you have to get in the car and go to the shops for it, you're less likely to pursue it – making the bad habit harder helps break it. I don't have biscuits in the house usually; it's an easy way to break my bad habit of demolishing a whole packet in one sitting.

Is your environment conducive to forming good habits or bad ones? Which habits are easier for you, and how can you make the bad ones harder and the good ones easier? Having my gym kit ready to go in the morning means I'm more likely to go to the gym later that day – in that way, I've made the habit easier.

The law of least effort applies, according to Clear. If we succeed in making bad habits harder and good habits easier, we'll see a shift. We also have to want to create the habit (that is, we have to enjoy it), and we have to have an environment that's conducive to the habit and a plan to make it happen.

The law of least effort is why it's easy to binge-watch Netflix. It's easier to let it keep auto-playing the next episode than to pick up your device and press stop. In this way, when we plan on watching one episode, we often end up watching the whole season and staying up three hours later than we meant to!

This is why I go on retreat to write books. It removes distractions.

I find less excuses not to write when I'm away in the countryside, in a cottage, by myself. I don't have TV and I don't take books; it's just me and my writing. I have to make it rewarding, though, so I take my favourite snacks and give myself a target. Each day, when I hit the word count that I'm aiming for, I reward myself with a cup of tea and some chocolate biscuits. That gives me that instant gratification; a reward that comes much sooner than seeing the book on the shelf. In this way, I'm forming good habits and making them easier to adopt.

I love the sauna, but the gym takes a bit more motivation. I go to the gym, and then I reward myself afterwards with a sauna, which is in the same building as the gym. I know I only get the sauna if I go to the gym, and once I'm in the building for one, the other becomes much more doable.

Another great hack from James Clear when it comes to forming good habits is something he calls 'habit stacking': adding a new habit we want to form on to an existing habit we already have, so we're more likely to do it.

As an example, I mean to take my supplements every day, but I often forget. Leaving them by the kettle helps remind me and make this habit easy, because I've stacked it with another habit I know I'll do every morning – my cup of tea.

Similarly, my meditation habit is something I do each morning for 10 minutes at the same time my partner is walking the dog. It means the house is quiet, and it's part of my routine before my shower.

Thinking about habits can become a drain – the ever-constant thought 'I must do this.' Reframing statements like this into 'the kind of person I want to become' gives the habit more meaning and also motivates us.

I want to be a calm, clear-headed, happy individual; that's why I meditate each morning. That self-talk gives me a different way of thinking about the habit; it's not just another thing on my to-do list I've got to get around to doing today. It connects my activity with my 'why': the benefit I'm getting from the habit and how I identify myself. It links my results to my beliefs. There's also the added reward hit my meditation app gives me: a gold star each time I don't miss a day. Let's face it, the reward of a calm, clear mind takes much more than one session to realise.

So, what habits do you want to form, and what's your plan of action?

Having the goal is one thing, but James Clear will tell you that the habit is the system behind the goal: it's the habit that will make the goal a reality.

Our fitness or weight loss goals only happen because of healthy habits. Our revenue goals are realised because of our sales strategy, so success is less about what we're aiming for and more about what we're going to do to get there – then the result takes care of itself.

This knowledge enables us to create a plan and develop good habits. I really like the analogy Clear uses of running a race. We tend to focus on the finish line, and ready ourselves for the result we want to see. But Clear tells us we should focus on being ready for the *start* line. If we're ready at the start line, the finish line (the goal) will take care of itself; it will eventuate by virtue of our training and preparation (our habits).

If I've already put my gym kit in the car the night before, I've already done the hard work; the chances are greater that I'll work out now rather than turning around and going home.

It's worth considering how you can make your good habits more achievable and more within your reach, otherwise your goals can become overwhelming. Clear advises focusing on one habit at a time and aiming for a 1 per cent improvement. This is achievable and still impactful as it compounds: Clear calls it the power of tiny gains.

THE POWER OF TINY GAINS

It is possible to achieve major transformations, Clear tells us, just by making small tweaks to our everyday routines. Although 1 per cent may seem like a minuscule difference, or one that is not even noticeable, in the long run 1 per cent at a time can add up to astounding changes.

Clear tells the story of the British cycling team in the early 2000s to demonstrate this principle.

Since 1908, British riders had won just a single gold medal at the Olympic Games, and in 110 years of the Tour de France no British cyclist had ever won.

In 2003, the team hired a new coach, Dave Brailsford, who was a fan of 'the aggregation of marginal gains': the philosophy of searching for a tiny margin of improvement in everything you do. The principle was that if you broke down everything you could think of that goes into riding a bike, and then improved it by 1 per cent, you would get a significant increase in performance.

The team began those minor adjustments, those 1 per cent improvements. First, they redesigned the bike seats for comfort, and used alcohol on the tyres for grip. They adopted heated shorts to maintain muscle temperature and used biofeedback sensors to monitor responses to workouts. The team tested various fabrics in a wind tunnel and had their outdoor riders switch to indoor racing suits, which proved to be lighter and more aerodynamic. They tested different types of massage gels to see which one led to the fastest muscle recovery. They hired a surgeon to teach riders the best way to wash their hands to reduce the chances of catching a cold. They determined the type of pillow and mattress that led to the best night's sleep for each rider. They even painted the inside of the team truck white, which helped them spot little bits of dust that would normally slip by unnoticed but could degrade the performance of the bikes.

As these and hundreds of other small improvements accumulated, the results followed. Just five years later, the British cycling team dominated the 2008 Olympic Games in Beijing, where they won an astounding 60 per cent of the available gold medals. Four years later, they set nine Olympic records in London. That same year, the first British cyclist won the Tour de France, and the team went on to win five Tour de France victories in six years.

One per cent on its own is nothing, but if you were to become 1 per cent better every day for a year, you'd end up compounding those improvements to create a bigger impact in 12 months time.

If, in terms of meditation, the most you can achieve is one minute, that's ok; the point is that you're forming the habit. Similarly, if you roll the yoga mat out and only do one pose, that's fine too: you've made the effort and formed the habit, and it'll grow from there. This 1 per cent improvement philosophy helps us take things on in a manageable way. Small improvements lead to big changes.

We've learned about flow and the impacts of deep work on our performance. We've also learned some strategies for mastering the habits associated with peak performance. What about the barriers to brilliance, though? What are the key challenges to peak performance and the things we need to watch out for that might stop us from achieving our potential?

THE BARRIERS TO BRILLIANCE

Now we know what brilliance looks like and the secrets to peak performance – surely that's it. We have the roadmap; now we can go away and be brilliant, right?

Well, if it was that easy, we'd all be doing it already. This chapter is the small print on the back of your brilliance prescription. This is the information that, despite everything we now know, can stop us in our tracks. I'm going to talk in this chapter about the barriers that get in the way: the hurdles that we come across on the journey to brilliance and often the undoing of our peak performance.

In this final chapter we'll learn how to spot the common barriers to brilliance and navigate our way through them. We'll talk about what's normal and what the research tells us the impacts are. We'll explore how to build self-efficacy in a way that holds humility at its core. We'll look at the difference between brilliant and perfect, and how our pursuit of perfection can so often be our undoing. We'll also explore some emotional barriers, in the form of fear and worry that can dim our light on the pathway to brilliance – and, of course, the impacts of change and uncertainty, so common in our modern world and yet more difficult than ever to navigate.

I've lost count of the number of people who tell me they've always wanted to write a book. It might be true that we all have a book in us – but not all of us become authors. This is down to our habits, but more accurately it's down to the things that stop us forming those habits.

What are the barriers to brilliance?

Author of *The Inner Game*, Timothy Gallwey, refers to the barriers to performance as interference. Primarily, they are emotions that get in the way of us achieving our potential. Gallwey's equation goes like this:

$$performance = potential - interference.$$

Gallwey's three emotional interferences are fear, worry and guilt. These are all barriers to our ability to achieve our potential and therefore performing. Gallwey believes that to maximise performance we need to minimise interference.

Whilst interference comes from our thoughts, it can also be affected by our surrounding environment, including the people and distractions within that environment. Gallwey advises us that an essential component to performance is giving our full attention to what we're doing (this is another way of defining 'flow', which I talked about above). He is an advocate for removing interference in the form of distractions.

Many of us can think of a time fear has stopped us at work, whether it be in applying for a promotion, speaking out in a senior meeting or something else. Where fear is concerned, our minds play negative tricks on us to keep us safe, but this fear can also keep us unchallenged and unfulfilled.

Fear keeps us playing small and mitigates the risk that, although legitimate and scary, often leads to brilliance. That fear might take the form of fear of failure, fear of success, fear of looking stupid or fear of what others might think. It might be fear of under-achieving, fear of over-achieving, fear of losing the comfort of what we have or fear of stepping out into the unknown.

Similarly, worry is something a lot of us commonly experience, along with anxiety. I like using the idea of the circle of influence (see the 'Sustainable brilliance' chapter above) to control my worries when they occur, and I also love the quote from Mark Twain 'There has been much tragedy in my life; at least half of it actually happened.'

Worry is an emotion that robs us of the present and also robs us of our potential. If we spend all our time worrying about things that have happened or that might happen, we'll miss out on the potential we have in the here and now.

Anxiety is an emotion that can exacerbate burnout and affect some of the good habits we need for peak performance in regard to sleep, exercise and what we eat.

Guilt is more subtle and not talked about so much, but it sits there under the surface for most of us, and it's just as impactful. It's one of the emotions that drives unsustainable work-life balance: the guilt involved in saying no, or not leaving early for an appointment, for example.

Before we explore worry and guilt, let's look at how fear affects us, and especially at how our fear of failure can hold us back where performance is concerned.

Failure is probably not a subject you were expecting to hear about in a discussion about peak performance. But when we talk about performance, we have to talk about failure.

Fear of failure can be so unhealthy it actually hinders the very thing we're striving for where performance is concerned.

I used to think that, to be successful, I just had to avoid failure – at all costs. Now I've come to know that failure is part of the pathway to success. It's inevitable that, being human, we'll make mistakes. I look back now on some of my past failures and I see that it's been the lessons they taught me that have led me to success – more on those shortly.

I'm going to go out on a limb here and suggest that, to achieve peak performance, we have to fail – and this is the opposite of what we're generally taught. Our society believes that failure is the opposite to success, and many of our organisational cultures operate the same way. They leave us feeling there's no place for failure, and therefore there's a resulting fear of it on our quest for peak performance. Giving ourselves permission to fail is so hard on our journey to brilliance: 'failure' and 'peak performance' seem like competing extreme ends of the spectrum – and yet embracing our failures is one of the most impactful strategies we can employ.

Giving ourselves permission to fail has recently been made popular by tech start-ups, and was much talked about by Steve Jobs. When we give ourselves (or our staff) permission to fail, we are granting space to create, encouragement to try, and permission to take risks and then bounce back if necessary, having learnt the important lessons.

It's normal for us to have a healthy fear of things that might kill us, for example – that protects us. But so much of our fear is *unhealthy* – in particular, the what-ifs and the worries about things that might not happen.

When was the last time fear stopped you?

Fear can leave us frozen to the spot, and it stops us moving forward. Fear is the main reason we resist change or doing something new: fear of what people will think of us, fear of the unknown, fear of losing what we have, fear of rejection and fear of failure.

But is fear always a negative? If not, how can we learn to navigate it, embrace it and, ultimately, overcome it, so it doesn't stop us from achieving our potential?

When I was growing up, fear kept me alive. I never walked down a dark alley late at night because of *that feeling*; I made sure I looked before I crossed the road; I checked the harness before I did the bungee jump; I moved away from the edge of the clifftop on a windy day – I guess I have a lot to thank fear for.

But then, fear is also the reason I spent too many years in a career that suffocated my soul, and struggled to leave a relationship

I'd outgrown.

Our fear of failure is what keeps us frozen to the spot; a fear of rejection means we sometimes won't even ask the question. But why do we fear rejection and the answer 'no', when most of the time we've nothing to lose?

'No' is our starting point. 'No' is the answer if we *don't* ask – so why not ask the question? It's the only way we can change that 'no' into a 'yes'.

We all fall sometimes, and we all fail sometimes, but the important thing is how we learn to get back up, carry on and grow into the people we are capable of being. This is how we unlock our potential and create brilliance.

> 'Failure should be our teacher, not our undertaker. Failure is delay, not defeat. It is a temporary detour, not a dead end. Failure is something we can avoid only by saying nothing, doing nothing, and being nothing.'
> —Denis Waitley, *The Psychology of Winning*

These words of Denis Waitley's were true for me in the context of the events I started to put on when I first arrived in Wellington.

I knew nobody. The events I was putting on were free – and sometimes no one showed up. I could have taken this as a sign of failure and stopped trying, but I knew I had a lot to learn about marketing and a reputation to build in a new city. I learned what I needed to know and I continued to show up. Four years down the track, I sell out venues.

I used to think that, to be successful, I had to avoid failure – this would mean success by default, surely. I now know that this is not the case, and it's changed my relationship with failure. I see it now as something that is inevitable and I therefore expect it and embrace it.

After all, failure is how we learn and grow. It's a step that brings us closer to success, and it's part of the path we must follow. Those who've 'made it' have failed and failed again – until they've succeeded.

I've learned that succeeding is less about being perfect and avoiding failure and more about how we embrace failure, learn from it and use it to shape our futures and grow into the people we're capable of being.

Best-selling authors can release sequels that flop, sporting superstars can have bad games and the most capable people can make mistakes. There are seasons to our souls. Some days, we are at our best, everything flows and we achieve great things. Other days, we can follow exactly the same routine, yet the results don't turn out how we planned.

How do we bounce back from failure, and use it to help us succeed in the future?

Every failure takes us a step closer to success. Ask yourself, 'What is this teaching me? What can I learn?'

I've learned to see the success in failure – not just the lessons learned, but the small wins along the way. For example, in the times when I've not been making money, I've been grateful that this has allowed me to focus on emails from followers telling me that what I've said has inspired them in some way. This represents a success in my eyes.

Those people who we perceive have succeeded in life, and those people who we aspire to be – it's not the case that they've done it right and we're doing it wrong. The fact is that they've already weathered the storms we're in now.

My first royalty cheque was worth less than $5US. My first book was a flop. But did this mean I was a flop as an author? Well, five books later, I can safely say that's not true – it turns out it was just that I had a lot to learn. So often we see failure as the end of the road – proof we're not capable of success – so we stop trying. In reality, we're never going to be good at something we've never done when we try it for the first time – unless it's a lucky fluke. We have to learn and we have to practise. Along that route we'll likely fail a few times.

Don't let fear of failure stop you even trying. And if you do fail, so what? That failure brings you a step closer to success: it's a lesson learned, and it's part of the path you will take to grow into the person you're capable of being.

Being brilliant always involves getting outside of our comfort zone, trying new things, learning, growing and challenging ourselves. Those processes are also where our risk of failure is at its greatest.

Giving ourselves permission to fail is probably the hardest element of achieving our potential, because we've long believed failure is the opposite of success. We've been taught that we need to avoid failure on the journey to peak performance; that it will detract from, not enhance, our effectiveness. Yet failure is the way we learn: we increase our capacity for innovation by experimenting with ideas. It's an inevitable part of being a human.

I like to talk about something I call the competence-confidence loop. Trying something new for the first time and leaving our comfort zone (for example, starting a new job or taking on a new challenge) is when we can fear failure the most. But as time goes on and we learn and grow in the role, and overcome the challenge, the feeling of fear of failure lessens. Competence breeds confidence.

It's normal to feel uncomfortable when we get out of our comfort zone: to worry about failing or about not being as good as people think we'll be. But when we try and succeed, we collect evidence of our competence, and this in turn boosts our confidence. This, of course, may include some rerouting around our mistakes along the way as we learn to succeed.

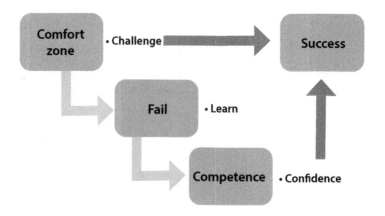

When we get out of our comfort zone, one of two things will happen. Either we'll succeed or we'll fail – and if we fail, we'll learn something that will help us succeed next time around (with the same impact on our competence-confidence loop). Too often we think failure is a negative – but it's part of the competence-confidence loop. We're just taking the longer way around to get to the same destination. Both paths can lead us to success.

When we get outside of our comfort zone, often enough our competence grows; there's then less that sits outside that comfort zone that we're fearful of.

I use public speaking as an example of this, because it sits outside of most people's comfort zones – mine included.

Because I've spent years as a speaker, people think it's something I'm naturally good at, and something I always wanted to do.

The truth is I was an author first. I'm an introvert naturally, and sitting by myself, writing books, was my comfortable place. Then I started to be asked to speak about those books. It was something I'd never planned on, and something that initially filled me with fear.

For most of us, when we're speaking publicly, our voice wobbles, we shake, we get butterflies and our palms sweat. This was all certainly true for me, the first few times I spoke publicly.

Our worry increases when people watch us, because we're

putting ourselves out there. We worry that we might fail, mess up or make a fool of ourselves, and then we worry what people will think.

The funny thing is, though, the more we do something we're scared of, the more comfortable it becomes, and the better we get at it. Our competence starts to help us feel more confident, and those nerves dissipate.

For the first year in which public speaking became a regular part of my work, I couldn't hold a microphone because my hands shook so much with nerves. These days, that's not the case.

Public speaking is just an example here; the principles are the same for anything we're afraid of: we feel the fear, and it may be hard initially, but competence breeds confidence and practice makes its better. Our comfort zone then expands to include the new skill.

A critical part of navigating our comfort zone and facing fear is accepting the challenge of stepping outside it – this is the only way we develop, grow and unlock our potential. The comfort zone is called the comfort zone because it's exactly that: it feels nice, safe and comfortable, and it's easy to stay there.

It takes courage to step outside our comfort zone and do things that are different and unfamiliar. But if we can move outside that zone, the zone itself expands, and as our comfort zone becomes bigger, we learn more. Things become easier because there are now fewer things *outside* the zone – and therefore the fear lessens.

PERMISSION TO BE BRILLIANT

We've talked about giving ourselves permission to fail as a way of learning. That's an inevitable part of being human – and yet, sometimes, we're also waiting for permission to succeed.

This is especially the case if we've been conditioned to play small, not to stand out and to know our limits. Sometimes we're at the outer fence waiting for someone to open the gate, when it's been unlocked all along.

I know I spent a long time doing what I thought I should because I wasn't sure anything else was supposed to be for me. I wasn't sure I was allowed to be me, or be different. I wasn't sure if I could run my own business, go out on my own, follow my dreams. I spent a long time waiting for a sign that it was ok to take these big steps into the unknown.

I understand why we have this hang up around permission. It equates to us seeking validation – the more we feel we have permission, the less risky something seems.

Since we were little kids, we've been trained to raise our hand and ask those with authority to tell us what to do. Remember permission slips at school? Permission to leave early, or to skip PE, or to wear something that wasn't uniform. For some, the need to constantly seek permission applies in adulthood too. This is especially true for women – and perhaps justifiably. It wasn't that long ago we had to have permission from a male relative to open a bank account.

For me this obsession with permission links back to the question often asked of those we worry are becoming 'too successful' – 'who do you think you are?'.

Who do we think we are, to be receiving that promotion? Obtaining that salary increase? Leaving that relationship? Travelling the world? Starting our own business? In asking those questions, we're asking for permission to be heard, permission to be different or permission to be enough just as we are. Can I wear this? Should I say that? Can I do this?

Don't wait for permission. Know that the only person you need permission from is yourself – and you can decide to give that permission at any time.

The same principle applies to the choices we make, the habits we form and our self-care rituals. You don't need permission to take your lunch break or request annual leave. You don't need permission to schedule down-time over the weekend because you're tired. Nor do you need permission to give yourself a break, do the things you enjoy or say no when you're overscheduled.

You can write your own permission slip. Giving yourself permission for taking risks takes courage; it's a real mindset shift. We're often more afraid of succeeding than we are of failing.

Permission to succeed is an outer fence that is a barrier to brilliance, but it's one we can remove ourselves. Remember, the gate is always unlocked – we just need to walk through it.

So let's assume we've all walked through the unlocked gate, out into the unknown, with our lights shining bright. What then?

SELF-EFFICACY AND HUMILITY

On the journey towards brilliance, a common fork in the road is our own self-efficacy. For many of us, accepting we are brilliant is new ground to tread. We've been conditioned not to be *too* brilliant: to remain humble and modest, not to get above our station. Often there's a worry that, if we outshine others, we're going against the cultural norms we've grown up with.

This is especially true for minority groups; it's why imposter experience is more prevalent in these groups too. We've been told for generations not to shine, and that our light is not as bright as the lights the majority are carrying.

With brilliance, we're aiming for the middle ground here: the 'zone of humility', as professor Adam Grant calls it in his book, *Think Again*. This middle ground, for me, is the acknowledgement and awareness of my brilliance coupled with the humility not to be an ass about it!

The challenge is that so many of us have been taught that 'humility' means modesty to the point of self-deprecation. There's an idea that admitting to having any strengths at all, or talking about your achievements, makes you a narcissist. In New Zealand we have a cultural fear of being a tall poppy (a because of the idea that successful people are resented or criticised because they are seen as superior by others).

Have you ever dumbed down your own successes? Maybe you've been reluctant to admit how much you really earn, or have taken the shine off a personal achievement to make it less 'big'. Usually we act in this way because we're embarrassed by our successes, we don't want to appear to be a tall poppy or we're worried about appearing as a threat to others. We might tell people we ran the race (but omit to say we came first), that we got a pay rise (but omit to say the bonus was based on top sales performance) or that we passed our exams (but omit to say we came out top of the class).

Following the publication of my previous books, I've become known as an expert in imposter experience

I've worked with thousands of people as part of my workshops, keynote speeches and coaching. I'm always amazed by the number of high-performing people who struggle with imposter experience and can't see how amazing they are. They don't recognise their own talents and achievements – which creates these feelings of not being good enough, and fear they'll be 'found out'.

We're constantly striving for success but always feeling like we're falling short; worrying we're not enough. To be successful we have to be more, better, improved in some way.

This takes our focus away from the skills we do have, the things that make us amazing and the success we achieve along the way. It breeds self-doubt and the feeling we're over-rated by others.

According to a 2011 *International Journal of Behavioral Sciences* review, 70 per cent of people think they're not as good as others believe they are, and suffer from imposter experience.

Imposter experience is particularly prevalent at work, and especially when we're taking on new challenges, a new job or a promotion. When we're feeling vulnerable or like we've got a lot to learn, it's common to have a voice pop up and say, 'Are you this person? Can you do this? Are you sure they've got this right?'

It makes sense that, when we strive for peak performance, we're likely to encounter imposter experience. It's the domain of high achievers.

Those with imposter experience have a tendency to attribute their success to external factors – like luck or the work of the team. We have an inclination to focus on our flaws, struggle to accept praise and think everyone else is better than we are.

Celebrities like Jacinda Ardern, Michelle Obama, Tom Hanks and Meryl Streep all confess to having suffered from imposter experience.

I remember imposter experience cropping up in my corporate career, in the context of my intellect as I got promoted up the ranks. I had left school as early as I could, and I didn't go to university. I wanted to get out into the real world instead: earn, travel and spread my wings. In my corporate life, I'd sit around leadership tables next to those with multiple degrees and wonder if I belonged. 'Who am I to question these people?' I would ask myself. 'What could I possibly have to add? I don't even have a degree.'

This self-talk fed into my self-doubt around my leadership role. It would result in me not asking questions or sharing ideas.

When I left the corporate world, the imposter experience didn't entirely go away, but it changed. When I'd go on TV or release books, the questions became 'who are you to pose as an expert? What if they ask a question you don't know the answer to? Who will read your book?'

Imposter experience can force us to play it safe to avoid failure, and work twice as hard to prove ourselves and not get 'found out'. We might not apply for the promotion in case we fail. We might not put our hand up at that meeting to ask the question, in case people think it's stupid.

No one is brilliant 24/7, although we put pressure on ourselves to be. We're not on top form all the time – but because we're capable of brilliance, we expect it all the time, and then we beat ourselves up when we fall short of it on our off days.

Overcoming imposter experience requires self-acceptance: we don't have to attain perfection to be worthy of the success we've achieved. We don't have to be Einstein to be a valuable asset.

I've worked over the years to employ the same strategies I now teach others to offset my imposter experience. I wrote extensively about this in my book *The Superwoman Survival Guide,* and I talked about in my 2020 TEDx talk.

So how do we find the balance between self-doubt and the challenge that comes when we think we might have too much brilliance? Well, we need to find the middle ground, the moderation of two extremes. We don't want to be plagued by self-doubt, nor do we want to be narcissists. The balance is the middle ground of confidence in our potential and humility in the way we perform.

I'm often asked in my workshops when we work on confidence 'what if I become too confident?' We worry that, by implementing strategies to offset imposter experience, we'll go too far the other way. It's particularly prevalent in our humble, modest Kiwi culture.

We sometimes confuse modesty and humility with self-deprecation. We assume that to own our strengths, know our worth and celebrate our successes renders us narcissists.

There is an opposite to imposter experience, and it's called the Dunning-Kruger effect. If imposter experience is being good at what you do but not thinking you are, then Dunning-Kruger is thinking you're really good at something when you're not: it's a cognitive bias **where**by people who perform poorly on a certain task overestimate their own performance.

Wouldn't it be a good thing to have this kind of confidence, people ask me? I respond by asking them if they like working with people who fit this description. Do they think of those people as good performers? Would they select them for a job? Invite them to a dinner party? You get the idea! Having low self-awareness and an arrogance about your capabilities aren't attractive qualities. Yes, those qualities may get a person a promotion (we can all think of someone who's been over promoted because of their confidence), but that person will be found out eventually, because they won't deliver; they'll be unable to perform at the level they've pitched themselves.

So, Dunning-Kruger sufferers tend to overestimate their own performance, and imposter experience leaves us underestimating the capabilities we do actually have. Dunning-Kruger is about illusionary superiority, and imposter experience about illusionary inadequacy.

Both of these are illusionary, involving a mismatch of our confidence and capabilities in opposite directions. What we're aiming for is the middle ground – an alignment of capability and confidence. To achieve that, those with imposter syndrome need to gain more confidence to match their abilities and those with Dunning-Kruger need to perhaps develop more awareness and be less confident in their abilities. Both need to be closer to reality than their confidence allows them to believe.

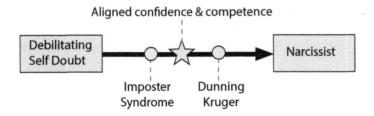

WHAT IF I'M TOO BRILLIANT?

That middle ground is where you'll find brilliance, too.

Then, of course, once we've built self-efficacy and found brilliance, a new problem comes along. This is the 'upper limit problem', as psychologist Gay Hendricks calls it in *The Big Leap*.

This term refers to that feeling we sometimes get in the face of too much success, or upon hitting our peak: a feeling that someone's going to come along and take it back; to say 'it was a mistake; you got too many dreams. Your light is too bright.'

The upper limit problem can mean we sabotage our own success when we fear we might be hitting our peak – when things are too brilliant.

'What if I fail,' we might ask ourselves, 'or even worse – what if I don't, and all of a sudden I'm taking up all this space and outshining those around me?' These feelings are common, and their cause can be subconscious baggage from our upbringing. Such feelings can lead to self-sabotage and imposter experience in the face of success.

The upper limit problem is especially relevant for many women. We're taught to be humble, not to expect too much and not to get above our station. We must tread the fine line of having ambition, but not too much; being brilliant, but not if it threatens others; and saying what we think, but nicely, so we don't offend anyone. Dreams are not for the likes of us; success should be hard work; we mustn't be an inconvenience to others; and whatever we do, we need to stay small, stay unnoticed and definitely not outshine those around us.

We can often hold ourselves back from brilliance because of these fears, but sometimes the fear of being too brilliant comes from others. We can all think of people in our lives who've supported our brilliance – encouraged us to aim high and given us that sense of 'you can do this'. But there will have been detractors from our brilliance too. Sometimes those who love us most can be the ones to have put a blanket over our light. Often this occurs out of fear, or love, and a sense of protection. These people who care about us don't want to see us hurt or disappointed – or in some cases, they don't want to see us outshine them. There are many reasons that people detract from others' brilliance – and some of them do come with good intentions.

Recently I moved to my dream house, just as my business was peaking and I'd married my wife. I felt as though all of my dreams had come true at once. I was walking around pinching myself, and I noticed a funny feeling – a bit of guilt and a bit of 'who am I to have all this? Is this too many dreams? Is it too brilliant?'

We're conditioned to play it safe and not to take risks. Our society has taught us to moderate our brilliance, to stay small, not to take up space and to deflect praise and recognition. We've learnt to feel guilty in the face of success and to constantly worry we're not good enough or deserving of success – we've learnt to expect that one day it'll all come crashing down, or we'll get found out.

It's a whisper in the face of success that says 'who are you to be here? This space does not belong to you – stick with the script.'

We need to ignore this voice of the past, and rewrite the script. Appreciate every moment. Yes, it won't always be easy – but enjoy being at the summit of the mountain, because new peaks come, and so do storms – and the chances are it's been a long sweat to reach the top.

THE DIFFERENCE BETWEEN BRILLIANT AND PERFECT

There is a specific risk high achievers are exposed to on this journey. We have a tendency to over-deliver; to want to go above our peak. No sooner have we hit the summit then we need to climb higher. Whatever we achieve, it's not quite enough when we're striving for brilliance. This is what I call the high achiever Achilles' heel. It's common amongst those who identify as perfectionists.

If you're driven, like me, to achieve your goals, chances are you're a high achiever. This can be dangerous ground to tread. It's closely linked to perfectionism. High achievers are prone to falling victim to our own excessive expectations.

We struggle to relax or utilise downtime because we are so busy – but also because we're driven by this need to achieve and be *doing* so much of the time. We can struggle with feelings of guilt or laziness about being unproductive if we stop for even a moment.

High achievers don't like to delegate, either: we see asking for help as a sign of weakness, and we assume it'll be quicker if *we* do the job – and probably better too. We hate to think of someone else taking longer or not doing it the way we would have done. This can mean that we feel like we're juggling all the balls life throws at us in the air. It's a precarious balancing act, and one that at any moment can come crashing down on us. Either we drop one of the balls or we hit a wall completely and burn out. I've done both.

For high achievers, balance can be difficult. How do we ensure we're growing, developing and pushing ourselves, but not to our detriment?

High achievers are always busy people, but if we're too busy, we burn out. We're also tired a lot of the time from all our achieving, and this means we're probably not performing at our best.

I've always been driven; I've always chased my goals and got the greatest satisfaction achieving them. I'm the kind of person who loves crossing things off the to-do list. I'll even add things I've done to the list, so I can cross them off and get an achiever high! Then it's on to the next thing. I'm constantly striving.

I've noticed, though, that as much as I strive, I never seem to arrive. Yes, I may reach my goals, but as fast as I'm approaching them, I'm setting myself new ones: something else to strive for, a new target, more, better.

There's nothing wrong with healthy ambition and a bit of drive to succeed, but not if we're constantly striving and never arriving.

In this case, we've set the bar far higher than it needs to be, and we'll end up with unrealistic expectations.

One of the ways we miss our brilliance is by trying to be too brilliant. This sounds contradictory, I know. Surely the higher we aim, the better our results will be, and the closer to brilliance we'll become? Not really. There's a dangerous point at which we aim so high we're trying to achieve something impossible, and we assume brilliance in a category beyond our reach. As a result, we end up missing the target completely. More is not always better. Brilliance does not mean perfection – because perfection isn't possible. Filtered photos are a great example. We feel like a failure if we don't look like a filtered photo in real life. But how can we? Real life has no filter.

A common side effect of striving for perfection is a misaligned expectation of what brilliance looks like, often brought about by comparison. We might compare our own version of brilliance to someone else's, or we might be stuck in the trap of 'more is always better', and what we're striving for is never enough to count as brilliance.

There is no brilliance blueprint that we can emulate or judge ourselves by. By virtue of being human, we're all unique, and our version of brilliance will be too. This reminds me of when I go to buy a new lightbulb. In the supermarket, I'm met with a wall of different brands, different wattages and different technologies. Most often I come out with the wrong one, even when I've taken the bulb that needs replacing in with me! All of these bulbs are capable of shining, but they're all different – just like us.

Sparrows don't compare themselves to goldfinches and wish they could be more beautiful – they just get on with being the best sparrow they can be. Follow your own path, and leave others to carve out theirs.

It can be hard to know if we've made it; we tend to keep

expecting that we need to do or be *more* to reach our potential and be brilliant. There's not always a finish line when we arrive where we wanted to be; no medal and no cold drink. Brilliance, in contrast, is a constant journey that we get to design ourselves – and once we know ourselves, the path becomes clearer.

Our culture has evolved to fixate on arriving – on results. We're always aiming for some far-off destination where we'll have more money, a better job title and a new house. The mistake we often make is to associate these things as markers of brilliance or evidence of our success.

In my earlier life, when I had 'everything', I acutely remember the feeling of it not being enough. My quest for more and distant shores constantly left me feeling like I'd achieved nothing.

When I was in Bhutan, hiking up a Himalayan mountain to a monastery, I asked the wiser, more nimble monk in front of me, 'how long is it to the top?' 'It' s better to travel well than to arrive,' he told me. What he meant, of course, was that I should slow down and enjoy the view.

If you're fixated on arriving at your destination, you miss the beauty of walking in the Himalayas. In fact, the walk itself was the purpose of the trip – not the destination. There were plenty of monasteries at ground level we could have visited.

Brilliance is how we show up every day, and that feeling of being present and at peace with all that's around us. We are brilliant when we're aligned to our skills and absorbed in our flow. It's not a destination we arrive at; it's what happens along the way. We run the risk of searching for brilliance our whole lives, only to find at the end that it was there all along – we'd just been too busy looking ahead for the finish line, or the summit of the mountain.

Just because we're capable of brilliance doesn't mean we'll be brilliant all the time. Nowhere is that truer than at the Olympics. Athletes at the Olympics are attending a worldwide event. The weight of their nations is on their shoulders. For many, it's a once-in-a-lifetime opportunity, and the training journey to get to this point will have been four years, or more. Imagine that pressure to perform!

US gymnast Simone Biles was one of many athletes who made the news in the 2020 Olympic Games for her decision to prioritise her mental health. She pulled out of an event after experiencing the 'twisties' − a term that describes the brain block gymnasts can experience mid-air in a routine, causing them to freeze or forget where they're at. As Biles has said, this can happen to all gymnasts − but you don't want it to happen at the Olympics. The pressure Biles was feeling, and the COVID-19 situation, must have also been contributing factors.

So how does this analogy apply to us? Well, we're all capable of gold medal performances − not at the Olympics, for most of us, but you know what I mean. We're all good at something. Some days we're at our best, but not every day. Some days we have the twisties, or our equivalent of that.

Biles' experience resonates with me. I'm not an athlete, but I certainly have my own less energetic version of the twisties − when my mind fogs, I can't think of words or I forget what I was saying midway through a keynote speech.

Some days I feel really productive. Other days I need to take a walk down to the beach and watch the surfers just to create space in my mind to think, because my brain is just not in doing mode. Some days I'm on form when I take the stage; other days I'm not at my peak, and I might deliver a silver medal performance instead. This is a normal part of being human. We often beat ourselves up for this, but it's to be expected.

Brilliance is not about climbing the mountain to get to the peak; it's about responding to the peaks and troughs that are the natural cycle of nature, like the waves in the ocean.

It's knowing what we need and responding appropriately to the seasons to our soul, across the seasons, the week and even the day!

I struggle in the winter months with my mood, my energy levels and my motivation. I want to eat and sleep a lot more (I actually think we humans were meant to hibernate!) so I know that, in this season, I need to switch things up and, in particular, to go easier on myself in order to get the best from me and give those gold medal performances more of a chance. And I need to be understanding of myself when I'm not at my gold medal standard during this season.

So often we experience this pressure to be perfect, to always be at our best and to constantly aim higher.

Perfectionism is the domain of high achievers, but it can be the undoing of peak performance for anyone.

If we're constantly trying to get everything perfect, we'll likely set ourselves up to fail. We'll also run out of energy, and this will take a toll on our effectiveness. As the popular saying goes, 'Sometimes done is better than perfect.'

Perfectionism can lead to some poor habits when it comes to delegation which further affect our performance. We like to have control over what's delivered, and we often think, 'If I don't do it, it won't be done properly.' This makes us reluctant to delegate, and we take on too much, increasing our overwhelm and affecting our ability to deliver quality work. This is ironic, when you think about the fact that perfectionism was the initial cause.

'Good enough' is no longer enough for us. But in holding ourselves to this expectation, we set ourselves up to fail. We expect too much of ourselves and lose touch with reality in terms of where the bar actually should be set – often we raise it far higher than it needs to be, and sometimes to a point that's impossible to achieve.

I'm a recovering perfectionist. I vividly remember that, in the early days of my public speaking engagements, the first thing I'd do when I got offstage was run through my notes and highlight all the bits I'd missed: the quote I forgot to use, the statistics I wished I'd included, or the points I presented in the wrong order. I'd beat myself up for these failings, even when the feedback had been great and the audience had given me five-star reviews. This was my perfectionism getting in the way of a great performance.

Perfectionism can be our fear of failure manifesting. Sometimes our self-doubt means we're so scared of not making the mark or falling short that we go above and beyond what's necessary; we work twice as hard, to make sure we don't fail.

The key to beating perfectionism isn't about accepting a sub standard job; it's about resetting the bar to a realistic level. We need to ensure that the expectations we're setting ourselves are realistic and we need to know when good enough is exactly that – a job well done.

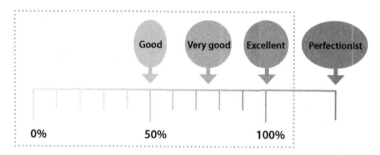

Whilst perfectionists will always focus on quality and produce good work, they take longer perfecting that job and spend more time and energy than is required to get the product better than excellent. In a society in which burnout is so common and we're all short on time and energy, is this really the best use of our resources?

If we're spending extra time perfecting our work, what is it we're *not* doing with that time? If we stay late to perfect that report at work, we're likely to be out of energy or time to be with the kids that night, for example, or tackle the other things on our to-do list still waiting for our attention.

Perfection, for so long, has been held up as the standard we must aspire to. Anything less is failure – especially in a perfectionist's eyes. Yet we can still exceed expectations without striving for perfection.

At a conference I recently attended, I heard Dame Jenny Shipley say, 'The closer you are to perfect, the less people will trust you,' and this really resonates with me. This idea changes our quest for perfection into something less desirable.

If you're genuine and authentic, I can trust you and connect with you. If you seem superhuman or not real in some way – too perfect – I'm less likely to. This knowledge gives us permission to show up as we are and know it's enough. In fact, it's what people are looking for from us.

The trouble with perfect is there's no middle ground. We're either perfect or a failure – and it's often our fear of failure that drives us. We fear failure so much we want to get as far away from it as possible – and of course the other end of the scale is perfect.

We set ourselves up to fail, because perfect doesn't exist. It's an illusion: an airbrushed photo in a magazine we're trying to look like, or someone's curated Facebook life we're comparing to our own, wondering why we're falling short.

If any of this resonates with you, know that being a high achiever leads us towards peak performance but it also requires awareness and balance of what's achievable, particularly if you identify as a perfectionist.

Top tips for high achievers:

- Give yourself permission to make mistakes.

- Stop comparing yourself to others.

- Remember sometimes done is better than perfect.

- Don't beat yourself up when you fall short – we're all human.

- Remember you can't pour from an empty cup.

- Don't expect brilliance 100 per cent of the time just because you're capable of it.

- Make time for self-care – build resilience.

- Leverage your strengths rather than trying to be good at everything.

- Ask for help when you need it, and delegate tasks.

- Remember the to-do list will never be complete.

- Remind yourself you're doing the best you can with what you've got, and that is enough.

MANAGING CHANGE AND UNCERTAINTY

Our final barrier to peak performance is something we've all had plenty of experience with of late.

Wouldn't it be easy to perform at our peak if everything always went to plan and everyone just left us alone to get on with our job?

Change is a constant; nothing stays the same. Yet when change happens in our life, we can be resistant to it. We like certainty; we like structure and routine, and when changes happen (particularly when they're not of our choosing) it can throw us off course. Our need to cling to the familiar and certain means we struggle to adapt to change.

This has never been truer than during the COVID-19 pandemic and resulting lockdowns. Weddings have been cancelled; big family events missed; families separated; and ways of working, shopping and travelling changed forever. We've been dealing with fears for our health and job security and the grief of a temporary loss of freedom for many.

I've never been religious, but I am a life-long learner, and I learned so many powerful lessons during my decade studying with Buddhists. There's so much we can learn from Buddhism, and other ancient traditions, that translates into our modern lives.

I've learned that, in the face of change, what's important is not what happens to us but how we react to it – we have a choice. This has been instrumental in changing the way I react to challenges. So much of what happens we can't control, and this can leave us feeling like victims. When we focus on what we *can* control we become empowered; this is where we get to choose.

We can't always change our circumstances, but we can always change our perspective.

As humans, we spend so much time trying to avoid suffering and chase after the good feelings. We want life to be good all the time, and we're uncomfortable sitting with sadness and suffering. This is why addiction is so prevalent: we attempt to numb the suffering and replace it with a 'high' – from food, drugs, alcohol, shopping or something else.

Other highs we like to chase after include the perfect job, the perfect house and the perfect partner. We chase after these things, and then when we get them we cling on to them and hope they never leave. Likewise, when we feel sad, we desperately want the feeling to pass, and to feel happy again.

Whoever we are, there will be a mixture of good and bad in our life. We all experience challenges; the good news is they don't last. The feelings we want to avoid don't last – but nor do the good ones. Everything comes and goes. This is the nature of life. The tides of the ocean come and go; the day always turns into night and then back again. If you're like me, you'll wish that summer lasted forever – yet we know it's always going to turn to winter. Thankfully, that doesn't last either.

But whilst suffering is inevitable, misery is not. Accepting the things we can't change allows us to make peace and move on. Good and bad will always come and go; sit with what is and accept what we can't change.

These concepts of *acceptance* and *impermanence* are central to Buddhist teachings. Everything will come and go, whether we like it or not. None of us will live forever; everything we have we can lose. This is why attachment, in Buddhist teachings, is deemed the root of suffering.

One thing we all know for sure is that we will die. There's no greater certainty. Yet we live like we'll live forever, and it's an utter surprise to us when we lose someone we love; we're inevitably completely unprepared.

Life is, perhaps, like staying in a posh hotel. We know we're only there for a short time – so we should make the most of the fine white sheets, the fluffy bath robe and free shampoos. We need to enjoy it, appreciate it but not believe we'll take any of it with us, because we knew right from the start we'd be checking out.

This doesn't detract from the pain big transitions can cause us, though, and the hurt of grief and loss.

None of us like to suffer, and yet suffering is inevitable. It can also be where our biggest lessons come from. During my time at Plum Village, Zen master Thich Nhat Hạnh's retreat in France, I read his famous book *No Mud, No Lotus*. In fact, I now have a lotus tattooed on my foot as a result of this very important lesson.

The lotus is a beautiful flower that grows from the mud. We too grow from our challenges to bloom into the beautiful humans we are. It's because of the mud that the lotus becomes what it is; without the mud it wouldn't bloom. Suffering is part of the human condition, and it's ok not to be ok. If we get sick or lose someone we love, of course, we'll suffer – but sitting in the mud is often how we get through those times, and over time the lotus starts to bloom. Sometimes our deepest scars can lead to our biggest gifts.

This knowledge doesn't stop us going through the grieving cycle – and this applies to any loss, not just the big ones. Any time something changes, we are losing what we knew and adapting to the unknown. It's a transition we go through again and again, and a process Elizabeth Kübler-Ross's change curve captures perfectly.

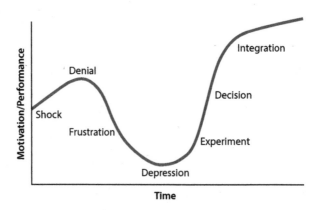

Whenever we enter into a change that's not of our choosing, it's common for us to follow this curve. It's a model I used in my HR days when we talked about restructures and redundancies and the likely responses people could expect when entering those uncertain times.

It's useful to know what kind of emotions we and others will experience so we can navigate through difficult processes and understand their impacts.

When we first learn of a change, whether it's a redundancy,

a relationship breakup or even, on the smaller end of the scale, a new system or a new boss at work, we can find ourselves in a state of shock as we adjust to the prospect of things changing. Then, it's not uncommon to feel denial: 'this can't be happening to me. I don't want to face this yet or think about what it could mean.'

This is followed by a range of emotions that leave us feeling anxious, frustrated and sometimes in despair (or 'depression' as Kübler-Ross refers to it on the curve). We can find ourselves thinking 'what does this mean? What will I do now? I wish this wasn't happening.'

We all take different amounts of time to navigate this curve, and it's not always linear. We can find ourselves going up and down the curve and back and forth as we figure out what's happening and process our emotions. One minute we think we've made our way through the anger, and feel sad, and then all of a sudden we're back at anger again. None of this is unusual.

Eventually we start to enter the upward curve into the positive: the more future-focused feelings. We've had time to process the change, and we begin to experiment with possibilities: 'maybe this could work; here's what I might do.' We then make a decision to accept what is happening, and finally integrate it into our new normal. At this point we've accepted the change and we're ready to move on.

The more time we have to adjust, the easier it becomes and the more likely we are to reach a place of acceptance and transition to the new normal – until it all changes again, of course.

This has been true of our COVID-19 lockdowns. One minute everything is normal, and the next the kids are home and you're not allowed out. And there's no certainty as to when this situation will end. As the lockdown progresses, we go through a range of emotions, and feel the impacts, until eventually we adjust and adapt – even if we still don't like it. Then, of course, the lockdown ends and we start the curve again with the new change that is our reintegration into society!

It pays to put some effort into understanding and navigating these challenges that can derail performance. We all have the potential – it's up to us whether we allow the challenges or interferences to detract from the brilliance that exists within us. Navigating these barriers is the formula for achieving our potential and performing at our peak.

CONCLUSION

As we come to the end of our journey, I hope you're closer to uncovering your potential. I hope that you have the knowledge and strategies to cultivate a mindset for peak performance and the habits to achieve brilliance.

I believe there's a unique potential in all of us: we're just too busy sometimes to cultivate it.

Replace busy with effective and quantity with quality, and begin to regain control of your schedule so that it matches your priorities. How has your relationship with time changed? Do you still use the B word?

What's your priority, your one thing today, this week, this year?

What about your energy levels to deliver on that? We can't be brilliant if we're burned out. How full is your cup? What do you need right now? Prioritise you, so you can refuel your tank and ensure you're a sustainable resource. Know your triggers and pay into your resilience account so you've got the funds for when the tough times hit, because change and uncertainty is part of life for everyone.

How we respond to the tough times is key, and this comes from our mindset. Are you cultivating the garden of your mind? Which thinking patterns are you watering? Have you booked some thinking space into your schedule? A clear, calm focused mind is one that can perform at its peak.

How might you create an environment, routine or habit that helps you do more deep work, aids your focus and gives you an opportunity to experience flow more often?

Feel free to go back through this book and reflect on your answer to the exercises: work out what you're now going to do with what you know. What resonated? What are the improvements you can make to your own life to ensure your light shines brightly?

My wish is for us all to experience more flow; to perform according to our potential – not as a watered-down, tired, busy version of ourselves or a person who knows there's more to give, but just doesn't have the fuel left in the tank.

If we go beyond busy and beyond burnout, what we find is a field of potential: a pathway to performing at our peak. When we can achieve this, not only are we happier, but everyone around us benefits too. Imagine a world where we can all give our best because we're performing at our peak – and not just at work but as a parent, partner and friend too.

I want us all to experience this: to know what it feels like when we've done our best work and still have the energy and time to go home and be our best with our families. I'd like us to experience the joy of slowing down and see how it helps us speed up; the beauty of achieving more when we've focused on quality rather than quantity; the ideas that pop into a mind that is clear and spacious; the innovation and creativity that become possible when we open up that part of our brain.

I hope you've been able to find some strategies that work for you within these pages. I also hope it's been a guide that's kept you grounded in realism: to know what's normal and to not expect perfection. I hope you can find that middle ground and know that part of being brilliant includes being sad sometimes, struggling with uncertainty and not being our best when times are tough. One sign of our brilliance is the way we bounce back and continue to shine, even when it gets dark. Go easy on yourself, and play by the 80:20 rule. Give yourself a chance, and know that if you fall in the dark place of a shame hole it's your light that'll help you see the way out.

Take one step at a time, and look for what works for you, because we're all different, and it's the power of tiny gains and your habits that'll lead you back to the journey of brilliance.

Now you've seen that brilliance is possible and that we don't have to burn out in the process, I hope this helps you acknowledge the strengths and skills you have to build your own self-efficacy and confidence, to own your space, shine your light and back yourself.

It is all possible – and I hope the strategies in this book have helped you unlock the secrets to making it so. Not just for your own performance and personal satisfaction but for the impact this will have on the world, acknowledging that we can all perform at our peak and be shining beacons of our true potential.

We'll finish where we started, with Marianne Williamson. She says:

'We are all meant to shine. … It's not just in some of us; it's in everyone. And as we let our own light shine, we unconsciously give other people permission to do the same.'

RESOURCES

Jess Stuart runs workshops, retreats and coaching programmes, working alongside you and your teams to put these words into practice and help you go from burnout to brilliance.

An imposter experience expert, she also runs lead with confidence programmes for women in leadership.

She is available as a keynote speaker for your event.

See www.jessstuart.co.nz for more details.

ACKNOWLEDGEMENTS

It takes a village – and I'd like to thank all those who made this book happen: proof readers, designers, editors, printers, PR and distributors.

I feel fortunate to have put together a wonderful local team over the course of five books – I enjoy working with you all.

To my loving parents, family, friends and my darling wife, I'm eternally grateful for all your support. I love you all.

To all those who listen to me speak and read my words: I feel privileged to have been part of your journey, and I appreciate all your feedback and encouragement.

ABOUT THE AUTHOR

Jess Stuart is an author, coach and international speaker who empowers people to be their best without burning out in the process.

A highly acclaimed event speaker, Jess has been featured on Three's *The Café*, the BBC, Radio New Zealand, Stuff, Tiny Buddha and Elephant Journal and in the *Dominion Post* and *NZBusiness* magazine.

With a background in senior HR roles and a decade in the corporate world, Jess believes tapping into your potential doesn't mean doing more or having to be different. It's uncovering what's already there and being enough as you are.

A brush with burnout in her corporate career lead Jess across the world to train with Buddhist monks and nuns. A decade later, after coming out, writing five books and running her own successful business, she shares what she knows about mindset, resilience and self-belief to empower people to unlock their potential.

Born in Leicestershire, England, Jess now lives on Waiheke Island, New Zealand, with her wife and their SPCA dog Minnie. Outside of work, she'll be found at the beach, on road trips, surfing, close to nature and the ocean or sitting quietly in the sun. A foodie, she loves dining out, cooking at home and just eating delicious food in general. A daily yoga and meditation practice keeps her grounded and gives her the energy for the work she loves. Regular trips back to spend time with family in the UK are a must for Jess, who considers herself a Kiwi now.